T0162534

Infinity to Dine

lazenby

Copyright © lazenby
2017

ISBN: 9780983243779

Library of Congress Control Number: 2017949903

Second edition

Sator Press
Santa Fe, NM
http://sator.press

The Slănic Salt Mine photo on page 36 is
licensed Creative Commons Attribution-
Share Alike 2.5 Generic and is
credited to Andrei Stroe.

Erwin Strauss is quoted on page 71, q.v.
"The Upright Posture," collected in
Phenomenological Psychology
p. 159 (Basic Books, 1966)

The statue of *Alba* by Georg Kolbe
on page 108 is licensed Creative Commons
Attribution-NoDerivs 2.0 Generic
and is credited to Chris Price.

The photograph on page 143 was taken by Jana Hunter.

@georgelazenby

For

A.,
A., A.,
A., B., C.,
D., E., E., F.,
H., I., J., J., J.,
J., J., K., K., K., K.,
L., L., M., M., M., N.,
O., R., R., R., R., S., S., T.

Contents

An idea's birth is legitimate only if one has the feeling that one is catching oneself plagiarizing oneself.
—Karl Kraus, *½ Truths and 1½ Truths*

Thomas Hardy's anecdote about looking up a word in the dictionary because he wasn't certain it existed—and finding that he himself was the only authority cited for its usage.
—David Markson, *Vanishing Point*

If we make a couple of discoveries here and there, we need not believe things will go on like this forever. An acrobat can leap higher than a farm-hand, and one acrobat higher than another, yet the height no man can overleap is still very low. Just as we hit water when we dig in the earth, so we discover the incomprehensible sooner or later.
—Lichtenberg, *Notebook F, No. 82*

Rich people who don't read are assholes and poor people who don't read are fucked.
—Sherman Alexie *(spoken in Baltimore on September 24, 2011)*

These questions were asked
between July, 2010 and
December of 2016 by
people who remain
anonymous
to me

.

How will we know if you've died?

That's the easy part.
How will I know?

At what point does reading stop being useful and start being insight porn?

I'll tell you a story about Johannes Gutenberg.

He was a very strange and secretive man. Before he developed Europe's first printing press he had been involved in a scheme to mass-produce concave mirrors. These mirrors would be set on a rack, and the racks full of mirrors taken to churches. These racks would be arranged such that the mirrors faced holy relics. The power of the relics, it was thought, would shine into the mirrors. The mirrors would then ever after rebroadcast a healing radiation.

After the mirror scheme went belly up Gutenberg turned to printing. He did much of his work on an almond-shaped island in the middle of a river. When he unveiled his invention many people speculated about the source of his inspiration. Some said it had been flatly demonic. Others said he was a Jew. The most interesting rumor involved a method of state torture and execution.

Pressing was a type of judicial torture used to force a plea or a confession from a suspect who refused to speak. To contemporary legal minds, a person was justly punished if and only if they had been convicted or if they had confessed. Because conviction must start with a plea and confession requires speech, a criminal could theoretically hamstring a court simply by remaining silent. To guard against this loophole, pressing was instituted.

The suspect was made to lie down on a wooden board and another was placed on top of their chest. Stones or metal weights were then arranged on the top board. Their number was increased day by day until the suspect pled, confessed, or died.

In Strasbourg, where Gutenberg perfected his own press, this form of judicial torture had a local addition. A thick block of wood was placed between the top board and the naked belly of the condemned. The block was flat on one side and carved to high relief on the other with the seal of the city of Strasbourg. In this way, as the weights were added, an impression of the seal was made in the flesh of the person beneath it. This was to show, after the person had been killed and their corpse publicly displayed, that the torture had been undertaken by powers legally entitled to command it.

It was said that this was the source of Gutenberg's idea.

I think reading is like this. It takes an exceptionally strong person to be exposed to the weight of truth that books can relate and for that person's mind to remain unchanged. There is a crucial moment for us as readers, which occurs just beyond the weight of truth that we can no longer bear. We die.

If we are lucky, and continue to read past the point at which our former self is crushed out of us, this will not be our last death. In this way we will always be able to cry out for more weight.

How do I escape anxiety and depression?

I often think about death. Something rivets me when I imagine my body falling through space. I am riveted when I imagine my mind clacking away like a knitting machine in those last few seconds. I wonder what my last thought would be. Or, if I do not die from a great height, I wonder if the loss of blood or consciousness bears a characteristic moment of re-alization. "This is the horizon of life," it would say, "stepping beyond this means you have left the world of others, the world where experience can be shared. Beyond this point there is only you, until there isn't even that." That feeling makes me think of the mo-ment on a roller coaster or a hilly road when you crest a rise and your stomach drops out from under you. And you are suddenly face to face with the sole feature of human life that is not subject to argument, because its experience can never be shared.

In my experience even ordinary people, people whose desires and movements through life never came into anything like a blinding focus, even these people become contemplative to the point of silence as they approach death. I envy them their focus. I wish the baited hooks surrounding me in daily life were less tempting. I wish that death could more strongly broadcast itself from the moment in my future when it snips away all my possibilities. The ways I imagine my own death do no justice to the unbearable radiance of the real event. But my fantasies of death are fundamentally idle, and therefore only the shiniest of the several baited hooks I fall for.

Depression is simply this hook when it is seated in your cheek. The line trails out of your mouth and up into the sky. Where it lays in the hand that holds the several neurochemical strings animating flesh. Anxiety is several octaves up from depression but the note it strikes is familiar. Where depression profanes the absolute and undivided truth of death, anxiety trades in failure, disgrace, shame, and destitution— the several social deaths it is possible to survive.

Whenever I get anxious, whenever I worry that I am being taunted, or worse, being ignored with justification, I try to get outside of myself. I 'know' that I am not repellant or embarrassing, but the objectivity of this knowledge cuts no ice in the court where I am tried. When the prosecutor is winning and the judge is his friend, I appeal to a power above theirs: chance.

When I feel anxious or when I hate myself, I take an oracle. The best oracle I ever received was from Google. I fed a Russian poem by Aleksandr Pushkin called 'The Prophet' into Google Translate. I re-read the last few lines of this machine translation when I need my case dismissed—

> And He cut my chest with the sword,
> and took the heart quivering,
> and a coal burning fire
> into the chest hole pushed.
> Like a corpse in the desert I lay,
> And the voice of God called to me:
> 'Arise, O Prophet, and see, and give ear,
> Be filled with the will of My,
> And, bypassing the sea and land,
> Verb-burn the hearts of men.'

I try to do what it says.

Why is everything so terrible in America? How am I supposed to like, *function*?

Whether or not you think you are functioning well, you are functioning. You are part of something and this something harvests your motion whether you know it or not. Knowing this fact does not make things less terrible, but it is important nonetheless to see the thing whose largest movements are composed of small contributions.

Imagine, for example, that the United States were a woman who has woken up from a 350-year nightmare. During this nightmare each and every cruelty of which a human person is capable has been performed. Performed relentlessly, for profit, for pleasure, to alleviate boredom, to punish others, and even, casting the tip of a whip all the way round the world until it strikes her own back, to punish herself. This woman wakes and tears herself from the grasp of these seductions. She has tossed in her bed all night long. She smells like sweat and her long hair is tangled.

She washes herself and this takes away the smell of sweat, for the moment. She brushes her hair. The knots make this slow and painful work. She works the brush through her snags, gently and patiently at first but then, in frustration, violently. She yanks the brush through her hair, bearing the pain and accepting the strands of hair pulled out by their roots. Finally she looks like herself, how she would like to look: like someone who could not possibly have the nightmare she's just had.

Combing tangled hair is terrible. Believing that there is a better version of yourself—one whom only pain and cold tears can reveal—is not a pleasant way to live. Unpleasant for a person, let alone a country. She is unlucky to have those nightmares and unlucky to have long hair that cannot be cut short. But as long as she can't bear to cut her hair short, as long as she must look a certain way—like someone who couldn't possibly have the nightmare she's just had—this violence will be necessary. The violence in her night-mare, a violence no longer literally present, will force her to pull hairs from her head as she breaks through her snags. All in pursuit of appearances.

Who can say if the pain of pulling out her hair doesn't migrate into her scalp, pour through her skull and down into her brain, feeding the nightmares that wait there for her to sleep again?

This is an analogy for how the progress of his-tory—a progress we might naïvely have expected to produce nations who accumulate freedom, wisdom, and self-knowledge the way compound interest gen-erates money—how this progress can be bent into a circle whose circuit must be endlessly walked. Half in a nightmare and half in desperate denial of the nightmare.

The helplessness you feel is the same helplessness we feel in nightmares, of our agency taken over by desires and dispositions we would never claim in daylight; the same helplessness we feel when we act compulsively, when our wills are directed by some-thing other than freedom—by, for example, the need to look a certain way. It's the helplessness of knowing that yours is a cellular contribution, of knowing any energy you give up will rise inexorably through a system of passages whose designer did not have you in mind, rise through these to fund the movements of a body whose insanity and self-destruction it cannot acknowledge.

To function for yourself, *as* yourself, and not some single cell in the weeping white woman out of whom this analogy is made, *that* would make things less terrible. To do *that* would be literally to embody the things we have naïvely hoped history would accumulate in the nations it breeds: freedom, wisdom, self-knowledge.

As ever, the answer is to become more yourself. To find the places where this woman's body has infiltrated yours, the places she has made you a cell in her own body and, by doing this, denied that you have a body of your own. Sever these connections. Read as much as you can, mistrust the opinions you can't remember forming, don't argue with assholes if it makes you ignore those whom the assholes are trying to hurt, cook your own food, and have nothing in your house that you do not know to be useful or believe to be beautiful.

Praise always feels bad to me. Is that wrong?

No, you're right to worry about it.

I find it difficult to deal with praise because there is something irritating about pleasure. Being told I am special or good at doing things right, this tensions me. I'm imagining those little rubber hemispheres we played with as kids. The ones whose pole you pushed in and partways inverted and then waited for the nipple-shape you'd made to snap back into a dome as it flew off the table. It's fun to be fucked with like that. But like anything that tensions you, the tautness dissipates and irritation takes its place. We cannot live at the altitude where pleasure peaks.

And anyway, it's a grave mistake to think praise aimed at what you've done strikes anything close to the person who did it. The arrow always sails far over our heads, on its way to the work. And feeling better about yourself for being told you've done something well is a little like running up to the spot where the arrow fell, sticking it in your chest and shouting 'You got me!'

How best to avoid describing myself in terms of the culture that I like?

It's good to remember the distinction between the things that lend color to your life and you—the translucent thing to which their color is lent.

Think of the Egyptian tomb Howard Carter began to excavate in 1922. I get uncomfortable and excited when I remember it. I find myself imagining the plates of carbonized fruit, the dice made from hippopotamus teeth, their 3,340 years of snake eyes, the mummified cats and the fillets of fish laid out to feed them—fillets found to have raised themselves off the plate into little arches as they dried and then suddenly to crumble into dust when they were touched.

The immense period for which the tomb's contents stayed perfectly still gives you the sense that time has been building up inside of it. And that the silence you hear once the doors are hauled open is not a silence at all but instead a deafening testimony that time is bearing.

The testimonies of culture are pressurized and can deafen us in a similar way. They are loud because life is hard. They are intense because disappointment can bleach. And for the person who needs to make a representation of their connection to culture these accidents (the hardness of life, its ability to bleach) can easily be confused with an essential lack of vividness.

But then I think of a moment in the tomb after the excavation was complete, after the cats, the corpse and his treasure had all been removed. In this moment a junior archeologist is alone, copying hieroglyphs from the walls. And the only thing he can hear is the sound of ancient wooden beams that creak and pop in the new air.

What the fuck is the meaning of anything? Why should I be compelled to wake up and go through the daily process when I'm just meat anyways and nothing I do will matter in a thousand years?

This makes me think about what happens in a woman at the midpoint of her menstrual cycle.

A woman's ovaries are, in life, almost completely white. They sit deep in a woman's hips, at the bottom of her abdominal cavity. If they weren't tethered to the uterus by a pair of strong ligaments, they would be free to move around the abdomen, like the testicles of a male fetus before they descend into his scrotum.

The uterus is usually folded in a deep bow over the vagina. The two Fallopian tubes extend from the top of the uterus like a person bent double, with their arms thrown back at the shoulders. At their other ends the Fallopian tubes are open to the abdominal cavity. These openings are delicately fringed with thin fingers of tissue.

By the midpoint of a menstrual cycle, one egg is about to erupt from its ovary. The egg sits in the middle of a ball of jelly about the size of a hazelnut. This is the follicle. The follicle is so large and so well-supplied with blood that it forms a black blister on the surface of its ovary. The follicle begins to digest the ovary's surface. This weakens the walls of the blister. Just before the follicle bursts it secretes a hormone that causes the end of a Fallopian tube to stir. The fringes begin to push their way through the abdominal cavity and toward the ovary. Once they've found it, the fringes begin to walk across the ovary's surface. They know the hormone that the follicle secretes and to discover its source, the fringes taste the ovary as they crawl across it. The fringes billow out once they touch the blister and then descend upon it like a circular curtain. The follicle forces itself out of the weakest spot on the blister's surface. The egg in its ball of jelly flows from this hole, into the abdominal cavity, and up towards the tent of red fringe erected by the Fallopian tube.

The egg is strained from its jelly by the fringe's delicate fingers and passed, from fringe to fringe, upwards into the mouth of the Fallopian tube. Grooves in the Fallopian wall undulate to conduct the egg deeper and deeper, until a swallowing motion along the length of the tube catches the egg and conveys it into the uterus.

In one sense this is where all of us are from but in another, this account is even more foreign than the most extreme alienations geography can produce.

When I say "I'm from Boston" or "I'm from Lagos," I mean to extend myself to other people. When I say where I'm from, I'm trying to help someone understand me. But this is not the same sort of understanding you could boast of having once you'd read how an egg gets from an ovary to the uterus. When we begin to understand another person, after they begin to talk about themselves, we understand *them*. If you read a detailed account of an egg's ovulation, you understand what *happens* to it. This is the difference between talking to a person over dinner and conducting an investigation to determine if they are guilty of a crime.

As thoroughly as we study the fringes of the Fallopian tube, when they taste the ovary's surface or delicately raise the liberated egg to the swallowing throat, we are only sharpening our account to higher and higher standards of acuity. And even a record of unbounded precision will never allow us to understand the egg as it is understood by the delicate fringes that search for it. When a person talks about him or herself, when they explain their accent, or unexpected turns of phrase, or the blackness of their skin by saying "I'm from Lagos," when I bow over my dinner plate to catch every word they say, they are offering and I am accepting an understanding of greater and greater depth.

This is because the kind of understanding we would like to have, for other people and for ourselves, is a mutual activity. Something is offered and something is sought. An egg extends itself and the roving fringe tastes in search of it. A person talks about herself and I lean forward so as not to miss a word she says.

I'm 21 years old, I've never had sex or any partners of any kind. Sex is something I actively want but would feel strange to actively "pursue."

Your instinct that sex is something it feels strange *to pursue* is right. Not in a moral dimension, where you might think it's wrong or douchey to hunt for sex, but in a deeper sense of strange.

It's a strangeness that stems from the way we're each of us educated about sex, and the fact that sex bears little resemblance to what you've been taught.

The words we reach for to talk about sex (before we understand sex) are words that make it seem discrete and isolated. In the same way you reach up for a product on a store shelf, sex seems like something that can be acquired. An *object* of desire. If you don't *have* it, thanks to your education in treating anything valuable as an object, you're impoverished. And in societies that educate people to link possession with feeling okay, nothing fills your cup with shame like being poor.

But of course this is dead wrong. It's wrong to think of your sexual status as merely the sliding spot on a line connecting 'Wealthy' to 'Broke.' Societies like ours do something much worse than instill this connection: they conceal the words by which any other relation could be expressed. These other ways are hidden by their seeming strange and different. And difference, real difference, is nearly as potent a source of shame as poverty.

We're taught to think of sex as an object of desire and so the satisfaction of that desire as something you have to 'get.' But in reality, sex is nothing like an iPad.

Sex isn't an iPad in exactly the same way being alive isn't a substance. There is no essence of life that fills your body but which is absent from the that of a corpse. Everyone used to think there was, that there was something you could distill from blood or fraction off of breath, and that the presence of this substance in medicines was what lent them their power to cure. Now of course we understand that life is not an essence you can isolate into a product. We realize instead that it's a process.

Same with sex. Fucking is change.

Sex is the chance to remake yourself on the anvil of nature. To remake yourself in whatever shape pleases you. It's our opportunity to unlearn the lessons we didn't know we were receiving. Every orgasm is a hammerblow and beneath the sparks you are malleable. The vulnerability of being naked with another person does not come from being close to harm but from being close to freedom.

When it comes to *wanting* sex, first make sure you know what you want to be. Because sex, just like the societal educations you didn't know you were receiving, will make you a way. And it will engrave you all the deeper for finding you blank. Because the world we live in has some deep-delving and extremely thorough ideas about what it wants you to be, and none of them involve you making up your own mind.

Consider:

In Australia, opal mining is conducted in a fairly primitive way. The opals are formed when silicate rocks are subjected to high-temperature water as it snakes its way through deep-underground faults.

Because of this the opals are found stretched over a wide area, as nodes in a spidery network of rock faults. This means they have to be mined by a scattershot method.

A prospector usually hooks an enormous auger to the back of a truck and drives it out to the middle of nowhere. He anchors the truck with hydraulic spikes and drills the spiral bit of the auger into the Earth. He sifts the hill of dirt and broken rocks the auger bores up out of the shaft. And he either finds opals or he doesn't.

This type of mining has turned vast areas of opal-bearing land into Swiss cheese. A land full of vertical graves ninety feet deep, and just wide enough to make sure you go all the way down. The mining has made a landscape where it's suicide to walk around at night.

Rock salt is mined in a very different way. Geologic salt is usually laid down when an ancient sea dries up. The salt flat this leaves behind is first buried and then folded into a corrugated sheet as it is compressed and distorted by the weight of rock above it. This tends to produce huge volumes of nearly pure salt. These masses can be equivalent to a cube of salt, a half-mile on each side, just buried in the Earth.

Formations like these tend to be mined in a way that turns them into architecture. That is, the salt deposit tends to be so extensive and so deeply buried that the only way to excavate it is to fashion a kind of subterranean building whose only structural material is rock salt. Salt pillars, salt arches, salt hallways, and salt galleries. The miners getting what they want from the formation creates—of necessity—something else: a vast and secret building, hidden underground and given definition by what has been removed from it. Like a sculpture.

So you can be out there drilling dry well after dry well, flagrant in your destruction of an entire landscape, all in search of a fourth-rate gemstone, or you can be otherwise and realize that beneath even the most featureless Kansan field a secret city can be excavated. Vast, unified, and private: far too majestic ever to be confused with a grave.

What are you afraid of?

* Eating something soft and unwittingly biting down on the tines of a fork.
* An article I read in third grade, during the Bosnian war, mentioned that snipers often aim for the isosceles triangle formed by the bridge of your nose and the two corners of your mouth. Bullets that enter the skull through this triangle almost always pass through the brainstem on their way out of it, interrupting the signals that control breath and heartbeat. A person shot through the nose will often seem to jump; their legs and arms will reflexively curl in towards the chest when the constant stream of nervous impulses instructing the limbs to remain extended is suddenly destroyed. The article said this was common knowledge in Sarajevo. Pedestrians often reported that

this triangle became flushed and itchy when they had to walk outside.

* That you can get used to anything, even shooting pedestrians through the nose with a rifle, if it is called your job.

* More than one dead house pet; especially the industrial ovens in which these are reduced to a collective ash after being euthanized by veterinarians.

* The trajectory of life that leads a person from being a child to being the operator of a cremation oven for house pets.

* Hospitals.

* Derision.

* The Sagrada Família in Barcelona, the dream of a crab raised on hallucinogenic host wafers.

* Crabs, but not lobsters. Lobsters can be vessels for the anthropomorphic substance humans pour into animals in a way that crabs cannot.

* Squid, but not octopuses. Squid have a sociopathy that octopuses are usually too intelligent to support.

* Celebrity in person: the monstrous energy that rises from the famous like a stench.

* Insects with mouthparts that suck or puncture.
* Swollen and inexpressible respect for another person.
* Small towns after dark.
* Policemen.
* The first coup of the Federal government.
* The painless knowledge of error just after a major injury.
* Bleeding that cannot be stopped.
* The freefall into poverty, as opposed to your life in it.
* Drowning: the need to cough that can't be answered, which grows more and more urgent until it consumes your whole awareness and entirely fills your last moment of consciousness.
* Your mother dying.
* Awards, prizes, public recognitions, and brass rings of all kinds.
* The back room full of pickled brains at a pathology museum, where the lights are almost always kept off. Does the physical structure of memory survive our death when the brain is preserved? These rooms remind me of diaries sunk into blocks of curing cement.

* Colicky frustration in public.
* Vomiting in public during the daytime.
* That there is no necessary connection between great skill and humanity (Ben Carson, Gertrude Stein, Ryan Lochte.)
* Being present for a preventable death you can't prevent.
* Narrow passages in caves that turn out to be too narrow to go through and too tight to back out of.
* Anyone in a position of power who hasn't had a deliberate, private, and extended conversation with a person who is homeless.
* Big black sunflowers late in the season after their petals have wilted, when the heads are so heavy with seed they droop towards the ground.

Where are you from?

Once I went to New York City with a friend. We went to the Bronx, up above Spuyten Duyvil. We went to visit someone who was housesitting. It was about ten o'clock in the morning. The sky was low and very dark gray. We took the Henry Hudson. From the shoulder of Manhattan I could see ice like gray flakes on the river's black leg.

The house was set on a domed lot shaped like a lozenge. The lawn was mown and everything else was overgrown. There were bare trees whose trunks were wet and a holly bush with polished leaves. The house had two storeys, white weatherboards, and no front. We walked toward a pair of sliding glass doors, up a brick pathway kneaded through with veins of moss.

The inside of the house didn't have a plan. It was mostly one, large room. There was a long, unfinished wooden table with mismatched dining chairs. There was a hanging lamp with a wide shade whose single bulb dropped a cropped circle on the surface of the table. Gray light shone through the windows. It met the yellow light from the lamp on a faded Persian carpet. The border between the two lights was lost in the maze woven into the rug.

There were plank bookcases on every wall. The shelves were simple boards painted pastel purple. Years of direct sunlight had removed even more of their saturation. The shelves were filled by hundreds of books. The books had been in the cases for such a long time their colored spines had each converged on the same tone of cream.

The three of us sat at the long table and ate the bagels and smoked fish we'd brought. The bagels were not sliced. We tore them up and draped the lox across the ragged ends. Nobody talked. When we'd finished I took the plates into the kitchen. My friend washed and I dried. As I left the kitchen I heard a tiny sound. I turned around. A little dome of soap bubbles sat in the mouth of the drain. The dome was ticking away into nothing.

The three of us stood in front of the bookcases and tilted our heads to the right. We called out the titles of books we'd read and the books we hadn't. We asked if this book was any good. Sometimes we pulled out books we'd liked and read the first lines to each other.

You went to New York one time, all the way up to the Bronx. You had a friend who had a friend who had a housesitting gig. The sky had been raining and the river had pieces of ice in it. You visited the house to pass the time and to see what a particular kind of adulthood looked like. The house was strange to you. It was up on a little hill and didn't care to be anybody's idea of a home. The inside didn't look like a family lived there. You imagined the absent owner moving wordlessly from this corner to that. You remember the basement bigness of the one big room. You wondered where they'd found so many unmatched dining chairs. Was it one by one or was there a store? Did they cruise the neighborhood on rainless garbage days? Is this what you did when you had hundreds of books but no kids? Was this what you'd do? Is this what you'll do?

You ate bagels and wished there'd been a knife. The cream cheese was too cold to scoop on broken bits of bagel. The salmon wouldn't stick. You offered to wash the spotless plates. You rinsed the plates under hot water and forgot all about soap. You squeezed a squirt of green soap into the empty sink and let the falling water work up a lather. Your friend who dried smiled at the deception.

Then they all read from books you'd never heard of before that afternoon. You remember wondering how they could read by light the color of dishwater.

On their left the wild ice ticked down south to the sea. Henry Hudson's parkway hemmed the left edge of his island and beetled up on the right bank of his black river. Their car hissed up the wet road threaded between these patrimonies. They crossed the Spouting Devil at seventy miles an hour. They drove a hundred feet above the very spot where red-nosed Antony van Corlær had been eaten alive by a pregnant shark before Dutch witnesses. van Corlær's nose was said to have been so red that a shaft of sunlight had once bounced off its surface, out into the river and struck a full-grown sturgeon dead. (The shark had wisely pressed her attack during a thunderstorm.)

The two of them walked up a slick brickway and entered an ugly house. The house was built on Jonas Bronks's kitchen midden, which was itself only the most recent addition to ten thousand years of oyster eating. These shells and his trash had built up a little hill. An eminent caterer to white flight had stuck a white house on the green crown.

The pair and a third remained in the ugly house all morning and all afternoon. Around one o'clock some hot water and a little soap flowed from the house, down the hill and into the river.

Why does it hurt so much when she doesn't reply to my texts?

Animals fall into two categories: those with rights and those without. Animals without rights exist at our pleasure, and we take it to be our right to do to them whatever we want. Microbes, fleas, mosquitoes, spiders, locusts, lobsters, snakes, pheasants, turkeys, pigs, cattle, etc. All of these can be killed or bred or crushed into fertilizer at our whim.

Animals with rights are pets. These are things like cats, dogs, cute pigs, horses, certain sharks, some dolphins and most whales. These animals are pets whether we have tricked them into living in our houses or allowed them to remain alive in the habitat to which they are indigenous. (It goes without saying that the Earth is simply taken to be humanity's largest house and the charismatic animals we protect by this fiction simply high-caste housepets.)

Anyway, the point is that animals exist by and large *for* us. This is because humanity is a meddlesome trait. If there is an arrangement of matter in the world, you can trust us to try and fuck with it. Domesticated animals are an excellent example of this tendency and the degree to which we cannot help ourselves.

Consider the most profitable breed of turkey. This is something called the Broad Breasted White. It has been so effectively bred for meat that its gigantic breast muscles prevent the sexual opening of the male from contacting that of the female during attempts to mate. Hence, every turkey you've ever eaten has been the ultimate product of a person holding a hen upside down between the knees and injecting sperm into her vagina with a pneumatic gun. This is what happens when the index finger of the human mind cannot resist probing the curtain of present possibility for a hole through which the future can be glimpsed.

I think animals show what we do to the external world and *represent* what we do to the internal world:

what we do to ourselves.

Whether you're shy or gregarious, your mind is an outward facing thing. Try imagining even the most abstract sequence of thought without the concepts captured in phrases like "what's before us" or "put that out of your mind." It is nearly impossible to imagine thinking at all without the concepts these phrases represent (here, 'what you need to focus on' and 'what you can forget.') This is because the mind thinks of itself as an indivisible point and one in relation to which all movements of body or thought are defined (forward progress, for example, is when we move "ahead.")

Now, how is the mind supposed to interact with itself when it is an indivisible point? Rather than worry about the fact that this is all a fiction we tell ourselves to keep from turning inward, we begin to meddle. In this way, other people (who presumably feel at least as self-contained and point-like in their perspectives as ourselves) become the subjects of our manipulation. When we manipulate other people we are generally making them into mirrors by which we can know ourselves. This is a good rule of thumb for understanding casual interactions but it is like a law of physics when it comes to intimate ones.

Our dominion over animals was meant to reflect the dexterity of our minds. In actual fact this dominion simply shows off the dazzling clumsiness that appears when we think we know just what we're doing. We dismiss this essential clumsiness as merely another problem to solve and so sleep through the lesson that artificially inseminating millions of turkeys every year would teach any sane species. Likewise, the lights we shine on ourselves tend either to melt or to cast into shadow those parts of ourselves it would be inconvenient to see. And so such realizations as we have about ourselves are like mice: fugitive, seen by accident, and very difficult to grasp.

In the end, it doesn't hurt because she hates you but because in the particular mirror that you've made of her it makes sense that she would.

The real question is why this makes sense to you.

Is Kanye a genius?

I don't know, but if I hated him I'd wish he were. To be a genius is a bad fate, one whose badness has been painted over by our present way of life. Our way of life demands constant production, productions of ever more sophisticated function and intricate design. That's the nature of selling in a market where consumers must be tricked to make them buy one more thing. In reality, the consumers know this, know that they must be tricked, and that their Consumer's Choice is really only spent on choosing which of the tricks they will choose to be tricked by. (Think of your parents telling you which Superbowl ad was their favorite.) Geniuses thrive in this swamp in the same way Hollywood runs on manic depression. Think of the energy that rises off celebrities like a stench. (Repellent and annoying energeticness is by the way the most common substitute for being a genius in a market economy.)

Borges said that genius was an ugly word ("nocturnal, Germanic.") I'd add that it turns artists into little Rudy Giulianies of the spirit: Officious little shits who snore their way through the lives of others, people for whom ambition is always quarried from their own native greed, whose creativity drips from the tip of a mental nose keen for the scent of attention; people who nurse an inner, weeping wound of self-hatred, a wound whose obvious and insufficient bandage is a bogus self-confidence.

These and other flaws drive these poor people to produce as much and more than any market can sell. And so they serve their ultimate economic purpose by setting the shoulder of their own tragedy against the walls of a marketplace; expending themselves in expanding it. But this isn't real genius.

I think people confuse the fruits of genius with its work. More and more I am convinced that 'genius,' in the sense that you meant, does not set apart a certain group of people, people with extraordinary talents or intelligence, but that 'genius' describes something much more humble: only a way of working. What you mean by 'genius' is *an unusually pure love for work.* In practice it is seldom more than an obsession with crawling further than anyone could run.

But nobody thinks of an orchard in winter when eating a pear in June.

Who are you?

The Sun, our star, sits at the center of the Solar System. Light streams from every point on its surface in unimaginable torrents. For us, 93 million miles away, its brightness has decreased by a factor of ten quadrillion. It occupies a spot in the sky the size of a dime held at arm's length. Even so, it remains blinding.

My father's cancer was at last undeniable when he held a curling strip of glossy photo paper out to me. He was seated at his desk and I stood beside his office chair. It was deep into Sunday evening. We were surrounded by dozens of binders packed with rare coins. His hobby made the room smell like dirty pocket change. I took the curling photo from him and he lowered his head. When his head was bowed, it seemed larger than ever. His wiry black hair, which had thinned in his forties but ceased its retreat soon after, was slicked back like always. The large knots of muscle at his temples were still prominent. I remembered watching them pulse from the backseat of the car as he chewed Dentyne on our way to school. The cinnamon gum was much too spicy for me but its sticks were his forty-year alternative to the unfiltered Camels he'd given up in 1961. I'd never been able to get his account of that moment out of my mind. He'd been sitting at another desk, cigarette cantilevered out between two fingers, reading the seminal, damning article in *The New England Journal of Medicine*. He said he'd gone around for weeks afterward pulling cigarettes from the hands and mouths of every smoker he met on his rounds.

The strip had three circular photographs printed on it and had bent into a loop in my hand. This loop was the paper's memory at having been stored in a roll. I straightened it out in the light of a lamp clamped to his desk. The lesion was shown in three angles. It was a pink crater that filled most of the round frames. A filament of blood trailed from the crater's lip and became lost in the yellow wall of my father's intestine.

I peered at the photographs with the useless intensity of a person caught in a lie. Then, a memory fell like a shutter. My father had just picked me up and put me on the counter of our kitchen. I was wearing mustard-colored overalls. The Corian was cold and I could feel it through the corduroy. My father told me to pay close attention to what was about to happen.

There was a tall bottle of rye whiskey with a neck like a chimney on the counter beside me. He tossed his keys with one hand until the Swiss army knife he kept on the ring lay in his palm. He pried out the blade with his thumbnail and used it to slit the sleeve of shrink-wrap keeping the cork in bottle's neck. He pointed out the way the plastic gave up its transparency to milky blue opacity where it'd been bent. "The chains are crooked here and scatter blue light. Blue is the narrowest light we can see. When you see it here, you know the molecules make a screen tight enough to catch all lights except blue." This didn't make much sense to me. I had barely been able to follow his definition of 'molecule.' (He'd taken a sugar cube and smashed it with the back of a teaspoon. He asked me what the mess was called. "Sugar," I'd said. "That's right," he replied, as he pressed his thumb into the bowl of the spoon and continued to crush the little crystals into dust. "And a molecule is the smallest thing you're still allowed to call sugar.")

He pointed to the surface of the liquor and told me to watch it very carefully. He held the bottle with one hand, careful to keep it upright on the counter, and twisted out its cork with the other. The cork shrieked and gave a low pop. The bottle's empty neck was suddenly filled by a white cloud. The cloud was so thick and had appeared so quickly I thought it must be a trick, cotton wool maybe. He held the bottle up to my lips and told me to blow across its mouth. I smelled the oaken sweetness of the rye. I pursed my lips and blew through them. The bottle let out a high and hollow sound. And as I looked down my own nose I saw a thin white thread crest the bottle's mouth and siphon away the cloud. My father said: "This was why they called it a spirit."

I studied the lesion under the light of his fluorescent lamp,

"How large is this?" I asked.

"I don't know," he said, "maybe as wide as a penny."

"Do they know the staging yet?"

"No, they'll have to do biopsies of the lymph nodes around it."

As it turned out he would not know the stage of his cancer until after the surgery. This operation removed the lesion, part of his large intestine, the southern tip of his pancreas and two-thirds of his liver. Stage IV cancer is any that involves near or distant tissue in the unrestricted growth of an original lesion, and is infamous for having no successor. I was standing in my kitchen when my mother called to tell me this. I walked to the window. I looked up and the only things in a perfectly cloudless sky were two crows. I very much wanted to feel nothing at all. Instead, I thought of a time when I had done something wrong. I was standing in my parents' kitchen with my back to the oven.

My mother faced me at the sink. There was a pink styrofoam egg crate open on the counter beside her. She groped for the switch to the garbage disposal so she wouldn't have to turn away from me. She ran the hot water, which laid a white noise over the whirr of the machine. Then, alternately yelling at me and looking back to the sink, she dropped eleven expired eggs into the growling drain.

The Moon, like every body orbiting the Sun, casts a shadow. The Moon glides on its route around the Earth, lubricated by the eternal grease of empty space. Its shadow, like an enormous, inverted flashlight beam, searches the void; only occasionally does this find the surface of our planet. This is called an eclipse.

My father's oncologist had invited us to a cancer symposium at Georgetown University Hospital, where the surgery would later be performed. Patients and their families, he said, often found these conferences demystifying. Cancer is a complicated disease and the medical edifice brought to bear on its destruction, no less so. My mother told me to walk my father into the convention hall. She would park the car in the labyrinthine garage Georgetown had sunk into a narrow lot along its campus' northern edge. We walked through automatic doors into a confusing building, and would have become helplessly lost in its many corridors were it not for the signs bearing a black arrow and the word "CANCER."

We arrived at an enormous room filled with rows of chairs. There was a dais at one end with tables and a lectern. The room was empty. He and I took seats in the front row. He lowered his head and knitted his fingers in his lap. I recognized this as his posture of endurance. He'd had heart surgery fifteen years earlier. The withdrawal from the codeine his doctors had prescribed had been so excruciating that I often saw him sit like this, sweat beading on his enormous yellow forehead, for hours at a time

There had long been an unspoken emotional truce between us. This truce is the form waspy self-control takes when one is raised, or married, in its citadel. His ascent out of ethnicity when he became a doctor. In the silence of that enormous room I asked him what would happen. Without looking up, he said: "I will get treatment." After a few more minutes I got up to walk around. I noticed a sign by the doors: "Surviving Pancreatic Cancer." We were in the wrong place. I told him, and we laughed at the emptiness of the room. We headed off down the corridor to find the others with colon cancer.

As we walked, I began to hear voices and the distant bruit of activity. There was a tunnel ahead. It nearly filled the height and width of the hallway. It was a section of large intestine almost thirty feet long. We entered a healthy colon but as we progressed the fiberglas walls became more and more diseased. Placards identified elaborately sculpted polyps, swollen diverticula deep enough to hold a child, angry red erosions caused by Crohn's Disease, a swallowed cocktail toothpick—four feet long—that had speared the intestinal wall almost up to its red cellophane flounce, and then, just before the exit, a crater the size of a truck tire. It was labeled 'Carcinoma.' I saw my mother leaning against a marble pillar in the hallway beyond the tumor. She sipped a cup of coffee as she watched her family emerge from the cavernous bowel. She grinned and said we were the handsomest things to come out in quite a while.

The symposium was like hell. There were three hundred people in the room and each sent up an invisible, boiling plume of desperation. A doctor in a business suit strode back and forth across the dais as he answered questions called out from the crowd. The room pulsed with the nervous energy of an auction. Patients stood and pled their case. The doctor would run through their options in a friend-ly yet clipped tone of voice. He kept referring to a chemotherapy drug that sounded like 'full fury.' The three of us sat at a round table with a middle aged Russian woman. Any good humor generated by the tunnel was smothered in this room. Our companion assured us it was possible to live more than six years with, as in her case, a simmering stage IV diagnosis. I could not look her in the eyes. They had been sunk deeply into their sockets, where they fairly glowed with a strangled passion for the extension of life.

Each year the Moon becomes an inch and a half more distant from Earth. The Sun is four hundred times the width of the Moon and, at present, four hundred times further from the Earth. The Moon occupies exactly as much sky as the Sun and can thereby obscure it perfectly. All total solar eclipses arise from this coincidence. In 625 million years the Moon will have drifted too far from the Earth for it fully to cover the Sun. Shortly before this happens, the final total solar eclipse will take place.

My father's surgery had reduced his liver to something like a third its former size. This remnant was unable to filter his blood of the ammonia and cellular debris that serious injuries release. His lucidity began to falter as these accumulated in his brain. A terrible childhood fell across his mind. He became too clumsy to tie the bows on his hospital gown and was haunted by black squirrels who chased each other through invisible holes in the wall clock. The roving, disembodied head of a dachshund floated several inches off the floor. Whenever I visited he asked me to make it leave. I said I couldn't. He would give a theatrical sigh and tell me to put a bowl of water down to keep it from panting at night.

When the sight of my father's unshaven face and empty gaze became too painful I would leave his hospital room and make myself find a new route to the parking garage through the maze of hallways. Once there I would take the freezing elevator down to its lowest level. Eighty feet beneath the surface it was peaceful. Nobody parked down here. There were only sodium lamps beaming out their calming, monochrome orange on the remnants of activity. There was an abandoned valet booth whose wear-polished plywood desk bore a ziploc bag full of losing lottery tickets, the torn third of a five dollar bill, and a styrofoam coffee cup holding half an inch of dark syrup. I found this scene very calming. In the hospital something seemed to creep up my leg like a vine if I stayed in one place for too long. It was the opposite down here. Down here the steel and concrete above me applied a pressure that liquefied my feelings, condensed and rendered stable my unbearable need to do something.

My father first talked about his solar eclipse during the chemotherapy that followed his surgery. He had slowly become himself again after his temporary senility. I'd sit next to him as he was infused with the contents of a half-dozen transparent udders hung from a steel tree at his right. Once in a while the robot would go past. This was a stout white pillar on wheels who rolled along a red line bonded into the linoleum floor. Its job was evidently to ferry chilled IV bags from the distant pharmacy that filled them to a brilliantly lit room near the chemo bays. Here a nurse would hang the bags in special cabinets. These were designed to bring their contents up to a temperature at which the veins would not balk. The robot said things as it rolled. Its stilted, distantly female voice would exclaim "Ow my feet are killing me."

I mentioned there would be a total solar eclipse across North America, from Portland to Charleston, in 2017. My father looked up and said an eclipse had made him want to be a doctor. I asked what he meant. He said there'd been an eclipse in New York City when he was ten. He'd snuck out of his family's house in South Brooklyn and taken several subway trains to Harlem. The eclipse was only total above 136th Street, he explained. In the darkness at noon on 142nd he made up his mind to be a scientist, later refined this to biology, to medicine, and then finally pediatrics.

We decided to go to South Carolina together in three years. At that time the five-year survival rate for stage IV colon cancer was around 8%. Three months later, with the whiplash that accompanies all remission, the oncologist discontinued my father's chemotherapy for want of any remaining cancer to destroy.

Just after we agreed to go South and see the eclipse, I saw the robot emerge from around a corner and begin its glide down the empty hallway. There was a line of large picture windows punched into one wall. The robot seemed to burst into flames when its polished body passed through the solid blocks of yellow sunlight, then become itself again when it rolled into shadow. This happened a dozen times as it moved towards us. It said, to no one: "How about those clowns in Congress."

I don't really get novels. Why does everyone read them?

You know that thing in a cartoon where the characters are watching a cartoon on television? And how the cartoon they're watching is always drawn in a simpler or more abstract style than the animated world in which they watch it? Or how a painter who paints somebody painting a picture has to make the painting-in-the-painting a little vague and not as sharp as the other things in the picture? Imagine the opposite of this: imagine a cartoon where the characters watch regular, real-life HD video; or imagine a painting where the person in the painting is holding a real photograph, not a painting of a photograph. Now imagine that it were possible to drag this relationship into real life: imagine that we were the cartoon characters and that it were possible to make a painting that would be to us what the photograph was to the painted person, to watch video that was actually sharper, more detailed, and less abstract than the real life you perceive with your own eyes.

This is not possible with a photograph or a video, but this is exactly what a novel is.

What is it with robots?

Imagine a person walking in profile view. One leg has just been planted on the ground, receiving the whole weight of her body. The leg on the ground is fully extended and straight but her torso continues to move. It has momentum from the previous step. The leg planted on the ground begins to topple. Her trunk moves off center and she begins to fall. Then she makes things worse. She uses her toes to push her weight off the straight leg and out past her center of gravity into empty space. After falling half an inch her other leg snaps out in front of her body and hits the ground. Her weight is transmitted to the ground through it. The second leg stiffens, straightens, and recovers the half-inch of altitude. Then the cycle starts again.

Walking is a process of continuously arrested falling. It's what happens when we discover how to turn this planet's gravity into the most efficient way of moving ourselves across its surface. (As is well known, above distances of ten miles nothing can outrun a human being. One hypothesis explaining humanity's early survival credits bipedalism first and our large, sight-hunting brains second.)

But now try minding it. Walking is one of the many bodily processes that neither requires nor long tolerates conscious intrusion. Breathing is another. Drawing every breath deliberately is almost as exhausting as refusing to take one (there is a medical condition, central hypoventilation syndrome—also called Ondine's Curse—in which the part of the brain responsible for the unconscious production of breath is damaged or congenitally absent. Sufferers are condemned to a life of choosing each breath they take and, when this becomes unsupportable, obligatory mechanical ventilation.) In fact, conscious intrusion into nearly any action the human body can premeditatively undertake tends to upset the unseen, delicate, and interior process by which we take any action at all. This is not difficult to verify:

Trying to walk consciously will destroy the fluidity of its motion. Trying to read by willing the eyes to focus and the mind to comprehend each word serially either boils away the meaning of the words or prods the faculty by which we comprehend their sense even further into obscurity. What is it about deliberate control that destroys our ability to walk?

One answer lies in the golden age of science fiction films.

Why do Gort (*The Day the Earth Stood Still*, 1951), Tobor (*Tobor the Great*, 1954) and Robby (*Forbidden Planet*, 1956) all lumber? Why are robots ponderous or awkward in our imagination? There are three ways of answering the question:

1. The first is the most obvious: they're all men in suits. Robots lack grace because the sci-fi movies that formed their stereotype were all low-budget. There wasn't enough money to make robots walk like people and so they became—and remain—stiff and hulking. This way of looking at the problem is perhaps the most literally true and so also the least revealing. But thinking about men in suits does lead to the second way, which is that

2. robots lumber because it is a reflection of their

internal nature. The characteristics that compose the robotic soul shine outwards and so create their physical appearance. Think of the classical robotic attributes: loyalty, pitilessness, strength. Inflexibility—in the sense of being faithful, merciless, or hard-fisted—informs how a robot should behave and so, naturally, how it ought to walk. Robots cannot experience or express subtlety and this fact expresses itself in their gait. This answer is better than the first but it still doesn't articulate what it is about walking that gives robots such difficulty. The third way is the real answer to the question:

3.   Robots lumber because they are not human. Walking is what happens when you unify the act of supporting your weight with your leap into freefall, when you reconcile your opposition to gravity with your submission to it. When this give-and-take between opposites happens very quickly it produces the illusion of smooth, lateral motion. Reconciliation of opposites like these into a middle way is a faculty that robots lack. This is because robots can have only those aspects of ourselves we can analyze and then consciously simulate. And walking, as we've seen, is the sort of thing we can't *think* ourselves into

doing. We don't "know" how to walk and so cannot program robots to do it with any facility. We can't even teach it: Children are not shown how to walk, they are encouraged to let go of the coffee table and—by a method of their own discovery, a method independently discovered by each of the hundred billion infants to walk through human history—cross the living room floor.

Making robots walk as we do is difficult. This is because the suite of skills responsible for walking are all so close to the heart of being human as to make their excavation impossible. Walking is an example of our ability to weave opposites into usefulness. "Our highest skills are contingent on the unification of opposites." This quote from a psychiatrist who studied human motion is profound because anything approaching an essential human quality—those qualities it would be useful to simulate in robots—will always remain in the corner of your eye. Imagine trying to explain why something is funny. Trying to point out something on the periphery of your vision makes you turn in circles, which is exactly what it feels like to explain a joke. Eventually you give up and replacing the profundity of humor with the profundity of existence. This is what is happening when we say: "You had to be there."

Another way to think about the difficulty of abstracting our most useful qualities is to imagine ourselves as submerged. We've been standing and walking for such a long time that those skills—and the opposites we unify to achieve them—have sunk right to the heart of us. They become separated in their long drift down and even infiltrate our dreams. The two most stereotypical dreams we have, flying and falling, testify to this. In these dreams our resistance and submission to gravity have been stripped from the cycle that walking transforms into forward motion and we experience the elements unopposed. Any human faculty that trickles down through the mental strata until it joins the aquifer of dreams will pose a challenge to automation. (From this it follows that the ultimate achievement of artificial intelligence will not be a conscious machine, but one that dreams. That is, if you can have one without the other.)

Language is another characteristically human activity in which the reconciliation of opposites breaks down. In the case of robots, the fact that we don't "know" how to reconcile Up with Down simply makes our robots clumsy. In language, however, the consequences of this failure are more tangible.

The World enters us and is immediately fragmented by language. In walking, opposites are continually reconciled. In language these oppositions live lives all their own. This is because they don't need to be reconciled with each other in order to be useful. While this is certainly a great help to conscious thought it has also been a tragedy.

Words like Up and Down are everywhere in our speech but the distinction is especially clear in the childish language of morality:

> We think falling is the pits because it lays us low and brings us down. You might get depressed or stoop to baseness if you are down and out for long enough. We would prefer to be on the up and up, doing super (L. *super-*: above, over, on top,) or even better, high. That'd be tops—pure heaven, (being high is sometimes tops enough to topple even the most stand-up guy, make him a failure [L. *fallare*: to trip or fall], and send him Down Below, to the Pit. Indeed, they have erected statutes [L. *stare*: to stand] against it.)

As language developed in us—rising through our mental strata until it outpaced our talent for unifying the opposites it contains—we became laden with a binary morality. Up or down: good or bad. This is one of the unforeseen consequences of abstract thought as English-speakers have inherited it.

The oppositions that flourish in language are fused only rarely and with incredible effort. When this happens it's usually because wisdom or genius has been at work. This is what things like wisdom and genius are for. They are the constant darners who mend the reality language leaves in shreds. They *walk* through the seeming sense that language gives the world, even as every other part of us stumbles. And when we try to use language systematically, as we must to program computers or robots, we very quickly feel ourselves begin to lumber. This is because thought that is perfectly ordered and explicit works against our deepest skills: those that feel at home within the irrationality of the circular and flourish amid the practicalities of vagueness.

Consider the first robot in English literature. This robot appears in Edmund Spenser's *The Faerie Queene* (1590). This poem (in well over 18,000 lines) narrates the adventures of several knights. One, named Artegal, is followed by a mechanical servant called Talus. This servant is remarkably similar to our modern stereotype of the science-fiction robot. Talus is immensely strong, merciless, and incapable of falsehood. It goes without saying he also has the moral intelligence of a three year old.

At one point in the story Artegal chases the bandit Munera into her castle and orders Talus to kill her. Talus recognizes Munera's guilt and begins to batter down her castle door with his iron flail. Talus' assault fills the castle's defenders with terror and in desperation Munera appears on the ramparts with sacks full of gold. Her men pour this gold onto Talus as she pleads with him to spare her life. The coins bounce off his metal skin as he breaks through the castle gate.

Artegal and Talus search for Munera amid the castle's cowering inhabitants. Talus deduces that Munera would hide beneath her stolen gold because she knows the robot isn't there to loot. Talus plunges his arm into a heap of treasure and pulls Munera up by her blonde hair. She kneels at his feet and holds up her arms in supplication. Talus, unmoved, cuts off her hands and feet, takes them outside, and nails them to a high post to warn passersby of the punishment given to immorality. But Munera is still alive. Talus takes her by the waist and, holding her out in front of him, climbs to the top of her castle walls and throws her into a river, where she drowns in mud. Later in the poem, after Artegal has been thrown into a dungeon by another villainess, Talus refuses to rescue him because Artegal had broken a contract with his captor, and was therefore technically in the wrong.

There is a connection between the lumbering morality—Talus' mercilessness and indifference—and the physical lumbering of the stereotypes that followed in his wake. Both Talus and all his descendants were made to mimic human skills that cannot be performed without the unification of opposites. The fact that Talus is a literary fiction shows all the more clearly the artificial nature of the thing he was created to execute: binary morality. This morality—robotic, lumbering, ununified—is within us because language put it there. And it gives us no end of grief as we try to use it in a world that can only be traversed on the back of an endless cycle of reconciliation.

The crude way robots tend to move through our imaginations—robots whose motions symbolize the unreconciled incompletenesses that grind away within us—this crudity is only the specific case of a much more general condition: the condition that caused literature in the first place. Literary robots are the logical conclusion of our need to pry apart the unity of the World as we perceive it.

This prying was the means by which the crystal stream of animal consciousness was first halted, then frozen, broken into pieces and the shards individually examined. This first moment of analysis—when a sensation was decanted out of the World and into newly-human memory for later inspection—was the first in a sequence of events that led to literature. We discovered that the World was fragile, was scored into infinite sections, that these could be fractured along a series of faults whose mysterious borders trace every last element of human experience, broken into things like identities, names, colors, ideas, ownerships, constellations, relations of amity and love, life, and finally, death. After discovering all of this we also discovered the pain this mental capacity causes.

The thing that literature attempts mimetically to create is the World before we smashed it. All literature, everywhere and at all times, is then at bottom a sort of frame wherein we arrange the glimmering reflections of a world in which we can no longer live. We do this in hope of repairing the continuum that was broken across the knee of our own intelligence. But these attempts are doomed to fail: no novel yet has unknotted even one person's foreknowledge of death.

Literature is simply the largest of all frame stories, one in which we attempt to breed a thought large enough to swallow ourselves. But in the very act of inspecting pieces of the former World, glued into the assemblages we call literature, we find the resemblances they contain resemble less and less the broken world wherein we must live. This is proved every time we look at a closed book in our hands after we have finished reading it, or leave a theater when the film has ended, and find ourselves stabbed in the heart by the strange sadness indigenous to those moments. This sadness at the end of stories rises up like smoke from a fire, one whose light can only be produced by the destruction of anything it would illuminate.

We cannot go back, and re-creating the world through literature is not a way forward. Literary robots, and their incarnations before this name—the two golden cupbearers of Hephestos; the bronze android of Albertus Magnus that St. Thomas Aquinas angrily smashed for disturbing his concentration; the various golems beginning with Adam who remind us that humanity is merely a robot made in the image of God; Roger Bacon's brazen head that could answer all questions posed to it but which he destroyed without querying; Spenser's Talus; Hoffmann's Olimpia Spalanzani; and everything else up to Karel Čapek's coinage of the term in 1919—all become members of an unhappy lineage by the light of this fact. Each of these robots, by virtue of being *an attempt at creation* within a larger effort of creative literature represent a kind of sighing self-awareness on the part of the author who invented them. Robots walk through literature as personifications of literature itself. And in this they cease to lumber. They walk somberly, in apology for the failure of human ingenuity to lift the burdens of consciousness.

Recommended a translation of the Epic of Gilgamesh?

There are a few things that make the Epic of Gilgamesh different from other objects of translation. The first is that archaeology has provided it to us in nearly a dozen, occasionally irreconcilable versions.

The situation is something like this: there was an historical king named Gilgamesh or Bilgameš. He ruled a city called Uruk, now in Iraq, around 4,600 years ago. This man either commissioned a personal myth of his kingship or adopted a previously existing myth as his own. This in turn becomes the source for all extant versions of the epic. The story was powerful enough to have been written down in at least three successive languages.

The earliest of these was Sumerian. This was

probably the first language to have been written down and may have been the language for which writing itself was invented. Sumerian has no clear ancestry and may be a relic of the linguistic era before our own.

Today, nearly every language on Earth can be traced to fourteen or fifteen mother tongues. This is how you move from English, to Anglo-Saxon, to Germanic, to Proto-Germanic, until you're all the way back at the last common ancestor of Sanskrit and the European languages. This last is the direct ancestor of around 585 languages spoken in Europe and Asia. That language, Proto-Indo-European, was last spoken around five thousand years ago. And there you hit the barrier separating what we think of as civilization from what came before: the Neolithic era. This means that whatever the painters of those French caves were speaking, we can be reasonably sure that it bore no relation to any modern European tongue. (The language of the Neolithic cave painters and that of the Proto-Indo-Europeans are separated by something like 20,000 years and 2,000 miles.)

At any rate, the idea is that Sumerian may have been a language out of this Neolithic era and this is why it cannot be related to any modern tongue. Sumerian might even have been a conglomeration of all the Neolithic languages spoken in Mesopotamia and so served as the language in which all the various Neolithic tribes could converse. If this is the case, Sumerian becomes exceptionally important in the history of civilization because it would represent the first deliberate attempt by humans to overcome linguistic—and presumably cultural—barriers for the sake of common purpose. Anyways, because of its importance to the first complex Mesopotamian societies Sumerian becomes the first language to be written down there. (Writing seems to have been invented as a way of keeping books and was only later used as a means of recording speech, although if you ask me a writing system that impresses numbers into durable media is already preserving spoken language.) The epic seems not to have been as elaborate in Sumerian as it would later become.

Then the people who spoke Sumerian began to speak another language unrelated to it: Akkadian. However, Sumerian still had a great deal of prestige attached to it and scribes continued to learn it as a written language for hundreds of years after it ceased to be their first language of speech. (In this Sumerian had a lot in common with Latin, which persisted as a common written language in Europe for something like fourteen hundred years after its last native speaker had died.) Akkadian is eventually written down, in two phases: The earlier of these tends to be called Old Akkadian and the later, some variety of 'Babylonian' (Old, Middle, Late, etc.) The epic exists fragmentarily in all of these varieties but the most complete version is in a type of Akkadian reserved for literary use. You can think of this as a deliberately archaic dialect kept around because of the prestige its antiquity confers. This is the language in which the real poetry, and a good deal of the immortal human resonance, get added to the story.

A professional exorcist named Sin-leqi-unninni, writing in Akkadian about 3,200 years ago, is the nearest thing to the author of the Epic of Gilgamesh. He acts something like a funnel. He collects and edits all previous versions of the story, renders them into poetry and creates a standard text. Nearly all the fragments of the epic created after Sin-leqi-unninni's edition appear to be copies or close derivatives of his work. This is important because the best-preserved copy of the epic we have is incomplete. (This copy exists on a dozen clay tablets, each not quite the size of a slice of sandwich bread, vitrified by the fire that pillagers set to destroy the ancient library where they were housed.) By paying close attention to the gaps in Sin-leqi's version it's just possible to patch it with later material. What you'll read in any translation will be the result of a hundred and fifty years of this work, by no means complete.

So it should be clear that translating the Epic of Gilgamesh is not just a matter of having a poetic ear and a good Akkadian dictionary. There are a huge number of textual problems, each of which requires a scholarly choice be made. Were the Sumerians smelting the iron meteorites that occasionally fell in the deserts surrounding their cities? Is this why the king's axe receives pride of place among his attributes, because it was literally celestial? And is this why heaven-sent Enkidu, Gilgamesh's friend, is referred to as his axe? And does this mean that whenever the poet talks about 'a stone from heaven' he's really talking about metal? And on and on and on. The list of problems and unresolved questions of usage would, and does, fill a sizeable second volume of any translation.

Anyways, all of this is just a long way of saying there is really only one guy who balances the huge knowledge of the language needed to translate the epic with the poetic sense needed to translate it well.

That is Andrew George and this is the ISBN: 0140449191.

What's your take on non-binary gender identities?

I think those identities represent one of the most important realizations it's possible for a person to have.

I'll tell you a story—

In 1877 a critic called John Ruskin wrote a throwaway line about art. He put it in a preface to one of his books about Venice. He said that nations write their autobiographies in three manuscripts: the book of their deeds, the book of their words, and in the book of their art. He said that all were worth reading but that the last was the only one worth trusting.

This is a profound statement. If you accept that the word 'nation' means 'the course of events pursued by a group of like-minded people,' then it becomes clear that Ruskin is really talking about *kinds* of thinking. He is making the case that human persons can think in several different modes, only one of which we would recognize as the rational style of thought (the one that leaps to mind when somebody says "I'm thinking.") Ruskin is saying that national deeds—wars or enslavements or internments of suspect races—are the product of one type of thought (one that imagines the world in terms of domination, power, and control) while the things a nation writes into its law, its ethics, or its philosophy are the product of another. The law is probably as close as you can get to rational thought crystallized in ordinary language. It is also our longest-running attempt to convert *reality* into an orderly simulation wherein all possible situations can be assigned a moral quotient. As this is achieved, it is thought, the law will crunch its moral numbers and recommend to us a course of optimal justice. It hasn't panned out. (cf. pp. 156–159, below)

So national deeds are the lizard brain at work and, when we drop the fluttering world into our bell jar to render its convulsions orderly and still, that's good old rationality trying its hand at writing on water.

These styles of thought represent the two great trag-
edies of human nature:

1. The visceral, unbounded joy of cruelty—the
   license and encouragement to act that the
   pleasure taken in cruelty seems to give; and

2. its twin, the bloodless seduction of abstract
   ideas.

It goes without saying that the world we live in,
its wars, its scientific domination of nature, its glee-
ful hypertrophy of destruction, its Kafkan puzzle
palaces, its determination to find the one, best way
of living and its attempts to pave that way with laws
and the bodies of dissenters, all of it exposes modern
life as a product of the first tragedy multiplied by the
second.

But Ruskin sees something special in art. He
imagines it as a kind of thinking the other, tragic
styles cannot corrupt or ensnare. Indeed, most of
what great art has in common is its ability to produce
a satisfaction that does not rely on domination and a
clarity that eludes the ability of language to explain.
We happen to live in a Kissingerian world of cruelty and power over which a checkerboard tablecloth
has been thrown. Most people take this prospect to

mean that if you aren't playing your life like a weird, unbounded game of chess you ought to be beating people up for their stuff. These terrible mistakes are precisely why it is so important to see art as a *way of thinking* and not simply another match on the table-cloth or struggle for dominance beneath it.

Art, as Ruskin wants it to be seen, is a co-equal portal of creation beside those of power and rational thought. Art is the door through which it is possible to glimpse a world that is something other than the vigorous hybrid of cleverness and sadism.

This distinction takes on a new urgency: Right now, in the shared cultural space that most of us call the world, good old postmodernity is pushing the continents of human possibility back together. This new Pangea explains, as the continent of Serious Things collides with and overmounts the one named Diversion, why our Batmen must be laughably self-serious and our Presidents taken seriously in the very same moment we recognize them as their own perfect parody. This compression was never a decision. It was always and only easier and cheaper to compress the several planes of experience back into a single sheet.

It's what you might call the vigorous hybrid's end-game: All news, all entertainment, all politics, all the cotton candy and every last bullet will be indiscriminately fed into the press and a new, universal medium of human existence stamped from these. The seething homogeneity of this medium is the reason we cannot take Trump's abominable past seriously, why we cannot maintain outrage at his deputized cocklords as their knives hunt for the heart of liberal democracy, and why those who love him do so as he does all this and more.

In this flattened world art becomes a means of carrying forward a vision of the future. Or, if art falls wholly into the service of the order and malice rolling out this satanic unity, it will become the perfect representation of life without parole. Naïve though it sounds—and at the very moment so many other things that feel worthwhile seem to die on our lips—in this flattened world art will become more important than at any point in the last thirty thousand years. And not just because the dry caves of the surviving elite may soon be our only subjects for decoration.

Art's example as an independent mode of thought allows us to see still other ways of thinking. Love, for instance, has its own order and virtuosities. People in love quickly find that it's as much a test of skill as anything else. Love reveals itself as a series of disintegrating stages. To have a talent for love you must ascend through these even as the basis of former affection begins to dissolve. In this way, people who are skilled at loving maintain the ability while it is crushed out of others by the contractions of a cooling lust, sterilized by the debilities of cynicism, or unmasked as simply another—mutual—exercise in power and cruelty.

Your body contains and articulates yet another organization of thought. I think the gender each of us ends up with (if any) is a reflection of how well, or badly, we are able to eavesdrop on the inner thought of our bodies. In this it has something in common with the talent for love—or art: A person who can understand what their body thinks is by definition one who also knows rationality and power cannot and do not exhaust the possibilities of life. Moreover, a person who has struggled with him or herself in order to hear *their* self is a person who will fight for others.

And theirs is now the logic of self-knowledge, a

logic for which the *intense* seductions of silence under autocracy and fascism have already been vanquished, by listening.

If you could, would you live forever?

Karl Marx wrote most of *Capital* at a side table not much larger than an open issue of *The New York Times*, feeling, as he did for most of his creative life, the pain in his side that reminded him constantly of his father's early death from liver cancer.

And besides, the phenomenon of suicide would appear to argue that even mortal life as we now experience it is too long for some people.

And besides, kites don't work without the string.

I hate 'spirituality.' Am I doing something wrong?

It's only natural you should hate spirituality. The word almost always refers to someone using the spiritual as spackle to fill a defect in him or herself. A beached fiftysomething with a face like a worn coin, suddenly terrified of death and enrolled in a community college goddess course. Spirituality doesn't flow in that direction. It doesn't give a shit about you. We are in its stream and even if we dream of waterwheels to harness the flow there's no anchorpoint to take a foundation. Most of the time we ignore the fact that we're going where it wants. This makes our situation invisible.

Infrequently, it announces itself. We are helpless then, and irresistibly magnetized. The Apollo Program is a good example.

Everybody thought Kennedy and Johnson and Nixon were spending four-and-a-half percent of the Federal budget each year to prove that America owned Science. This was all a fiction. The Apollo Program was an elaborate demonstration of how even the blandest among us are under the heel of the spirit.

NASA needed astronauts to plant a flag on the Moon. For obvious reasons the astronauts selected were the most reliable type of man America makes: white, straight, center-right and full-starch protestant, each spawned from the union of science and the military. Every last one of them the heart of the heart of the TV dinner demographic. But then they get shot into space.

They are tossed from the gravity of this planet, tossed across a quarter-million miles of nothing, to be snatched by the Moon after three days of coasting. Eighteen guys did this and twelve descended further to discover the Moon smells like a recently fired gun.

Every last one of them came back irrevocably changed. America had sent the squarest men it could find to the Moon and the Moon sent back humans.

Armstrong became a teacher, then a farmer. Alan Bean became a painter. Edgar Mitchell started believing in UFOs. Along the way he also managed to crystallize the experience of seeing your entire home planet at once—

> You develop an instant global consciousness, a people orientation, an intense dissatisfaction with the state of the world, and a compulsion to do something about it. From out there on the Moon, international politics look so petty. You want to grab a politician by the scruff of the neck and drag him a quarter-million miles out and say, "Look at that, you son of a bitch."
>
> (*People*: April 8th, 1974)

Will you tell me a story?

Baby has green eyes. She is securely planted in the seat designed to hold babies. Her mother pushes the cart. They move plow-wise through the aisles of the supermarket. BOUSTROPHEDON–10¢, is grabbed from a hanging vine of impulse products. It caroms off two walls before settling in the empty basket behind baby. The mother consults a list and runs an index finger across the faces of several HOT SHAME WITH HARD LUMPS IN THROAT–$3.99/. She weighs one in her hand and probes its surface with a painted nail. Still hard; in the cart. The mother stares into space and her mouth hangs open. She jerks. She looks back at the list and knocks out three more items, sold as one. THE

FINGERS DRAWING TICKS AND HISSES FROM SCREEN OF JUST-EXTINGUISHED TELEVISION TUBE; THE SMELL OF BURPS WHEN BELCHED AFTER ACCIDENTALLY SWALLOWING POOL WATER; DIMPLES, RED AND WHITE, ON KNEECAPS, IMPRESSED BY CARPET PILE—99¢. The trio clatter into the basket. Baby raises both arms and tilts her head far back into the tuck of fat at the nape of her neck. She goggles at the dashed line of lights above the aisle. The mother faces a tantalizing deal. MEN'S SLACKS, BUNCHED IN HOT FISTS, BECOMING MOIST—Free with any purchase of YELLOW CHEEKS AND A BONE WHITE NOSE, GLIMPSED FROM BEHIND A TALL THIGH, THROUGH STINGING EYES PLUS THE MALTY SMELL OF UNBATHED PATIENT—$8.99. The mother heaves these from their shelf until they balance on the rim of the cart. She weaves her fingers through the cart's metal mesh and an inelegant shove from one hip sends them in. They land, upside down, on the HOT SHAME. Baby jerks and shrugs at the sound over her shoulder. The mother glances at her watch and curses. She pockets her list and curses again. Baby's green eyes widen and her head swivels unsteadily as she tracks her mother crossing the aisle. The mother snatches at random from a bank of scents. Each is passed behind her back and dropped into the cart without consulting prices: RAPIER-SHARP NEW CAR TIRES; STALE MENSES ON MOTHER'S CLOTHES; BILE IN DIAPERS; ROTTING PRAWNS IN CAT YAWN; SOUR BREAST MILK; HOT COOK- IE EXHAUST FROM LABORING VACUUM CLEANER MOTOR; THE AIR INSIDE A BABYDOLL'S HEAD; ELMER'S GLUE; NEW DECK OF CARDS; MOTHBALLS AND OLD HEAT IN ATTIC; SWEATY HANDS AF- TER HOLDING PENNIES; MOSSY CREEK; UNWASHED LUNCHBOX; HOSPITAL; ROASTED GRAIN OF FRESH URINE; MALTY SHEETS IN EMPTY BED; FORM- ALDEHYDE; FARTY NATURAL GAS LEAK; NAPTHA OF GRANDMOTHER'S DENTAL TARTAR; BURLAP COFFEE SACKS AND HESSIAN VERTICAL GYM ROPES; HOT WET PIZZA CARDBOARD; EGGY HAIR- CURLERS AND STRAIGHTENING WANDS;

THE INSIDES OF PIANOS AND GRAND-
FATHER CLOCKS; FRESH MENSES; ICE
CREAM PARLOR; BAKED PINE BOARDS
AND COCONUT OIL IN BEACH HOUSE;
MARIJUANA SMOKE IN UNWASHED
HAIR; SIMMERING JACUZZI BROTH;
THE BATHROOM AFTER A SMOKER HAS
SHOWERED; BACKSTAGE SAWDUST AND
PEPPERY BLACK VELVET CURTAINS;
OZONE ON NEW PHOTOCOPIES; FRUITY
BALLPOINT PEN INK; TESTING CENTER
CHAIR SEAT; THE ANISE IN PHỞ; BEER
SPILLED ON DIRT; CHLORINATED EMPTI-
NESS OF SAFFRON STRANDS; DECAYING
COLLAGE MATERIAL IN MODERN ART
GALLERY; AIRPLANE GLUE OF SNORT-
ED COCAINE; SOFTENING VARNISH IN
LATE NIGHT BAR; FRESH TOILET WA-
TER; SICKBED; RESOLVING HEADCOLD;
IKEA WAREHOUSE FULL OF FLATPAK;
HOUSEGUEST; DIRTY SPONGE; MANURE
IN FRESH MULCH THAT STEAMS IN
THE MORNING; VEGETARIAN SWEAT
OF YOGA STUDIO; MULTIVITAMIN PILL

BOTTLE; HAIR IN DIRECT SUNLIGHT; REALTOR'S ONLY BLAZER; HISTRIONIC CANDLE SHOPPE; SEX; VOMIT; IODINE; YEASTY BABY; CHARRING JACKOLAN-TERN; MOLDY TOWEL; MUNICIPAL WA-TER; GUNSMOKE.

Do you want to be famous?

In 1928 the architect Mies van der Rohe was commissioned to design a pavilion representing Weimar Germany at the 1929 International Exhibition in Barcelona. The building became justly famous as the most eloquent definition of what was later gathered into architectural Modernism. This definition was something like: 'Not only doing much more with far less, but becoming so good at it you can thread a way out of the bewilderment and perversity that gnaw at modern lives, lives apparently filled with unparalleled bounty and convenience.'

The pavilion was designed to be doorless and made mostly of glass. In almost every way a building could be optimistic for the century it wanted to predict, this one was. The evidence of class oppression that great houses bear—things like backstairs and basement kitchens—are gone. Blank walls on which the evidence of wealth could be displayed have been replaced by windows. Reality is the thing transparent walls force your attention to confront. The pavilion even did away with the convention of a 'front' or a 'back.' Duplicity becomes more difficult than simply being honest without a face on which to project how we want to be seen. The building hopes that without anything to hide behind, the very ideas of secrecy and guile will become too cumbersome to survive.

But like the man said, in the very temple of delight melancholy has her sovereign shrine. There was one place in the pavilion that showed a terrible shadow falling across the 20th century. Beyond the main room there was a reflecting pool. In the middle of the pool stood a statue of a nude woman. The choice to place a statue at a remove from anyone who would look at it is as elegant a definition as anything else in the building, but what is being defined is hideous. A statue has been taken out of the round and placed in a position that allows only one point of view. This is an example of something our era has done on an industrial scale—the reduction of volumes to images. By definition a statue fills a volume, but limiting our perspective makes it flat: an image.

Degenerating the freedom to see from whichever perspective suits you, down to only one, is as old as the allegory of the cave, where statues were reduced to their shadows. But the pavilion predicts this process will come to dominate everything the statue represents: Art, diversion, beauty, and eventually, people themselves. All of us will buy, favor, love, and appreciate from across an uncrossable distance. We will be segregated from everything we admire and from everything we want because images are all we'll be served and flatness cannot be embraced.

Fame towers over and above every other example of this process. If we are tricked by advertising into buying a phantom, wanting to be famous is wanting to become that phantom. To trade a meal for the smell of a meal. It's a desire that mistakes isolation for rarity, distance for height, and loneliness for being exceptional. The popular desire for fame is the crowning achievement of a hundred year campaign to iron out any aspect of being alive that calls for a complex and irreducible expression of humanity.

And this fails to deter those who would gladly lay with an iron in hopes of becoming fuller.

What do you think about Steve Jobs?

One of Heraclitus' best lines turns on a pun. In the archaic dialect of Greek that Homer used, the word for an archer's bow is 'bios' (βιός). The Greek word for 'life' is spelled the same way (βίος). Heraclitus' line runs—

βιός τῷ τόξῳ ὄνομα βίος ἔργον δὲ θάνατος
The name of the bow is life but its work is death.

This is the first and the last word on technology.

Technology is cleverness at play in the material world. It seeks to improve life by the manipulation of unthinking matter. But, because there is nothing less intelligent than cleverness, these manipulations take place wholly by the light of death. Technology is to death what the gold ingot is to the thousand tons of ore. Every attempt to improve the present conditions of life by technological means is a further tribute laid at the feet of death as he sits in the absolute sovereignty this activity grants him.

Any hyperbole here will quickly drain away when you imagine what an immortal version of yourself might be like. Would a you who could not die augment anything about the body? Would that immortal person need a car or a ship when walking and swimming can be indefinitely sustained? Would events and feelings—whose details could never be obliterated—need to be committed to paper? Would time itself even exist, to say nothing of needing keeping, to a you whom change could not alter? And if space and time become irrelevancies, of what possible interest is manipulating the dead matter that fills these domains?

What we call 'technology' is then a kind of textile. A thread of cleverness crossing the threat of death. We are clothed in the fabric this technique creates; we wear it like a better skin to keep out the several chills that mortal life is born to. But the chill is woven in.

One of the better films about technology seems to have been made with Heraclitus' insight in mind. If you've ever looked into Homer's Odyssey you may remember that the weapon associated with Odysseus is the bow. In *2001: A Space Odyssey*, death is the first and second use to which technology is put. The monolith reveals something to the ape-men and soon they club tapirs and each other to death. A later protagonist of the film, called Bowman, uses a smaller club to kill a machine. A machine that murdered men when it first realized it could die.

The intimacy with which death penetrates technology is something more often felt than realized. This intimacy is why a robot seems more and more like a living corpse as its appearance approaches that of human flesh; why a dying person seems to die twice as much when a machine pumps air in and out of their lungs through a corrugated tube threaded down their throat. It is this intimacy that cloaked the death of Steve Jobs in an aura his death could never otherwise have assumed.

Steve Jobs came to represent the mirage of eternal life that shimmers across the face of technology when death is so closely woven into it as to make distinction impossible. *This* is the mirage that makes the bow life when its work is death. It is what the monolith whispered to the ape-men, the advice that made them kill to eat meat and kill to drink water; it is what men, in turn, whispered to HAL and what Bowman was born knowing.

When Jobs died of cancer the air became momentarily clear. The mirage flickered and then it vanished. The world seemed to grieve for a man it did not know, but this grief was what the hands felt when the hem of what we have become frayed just enough to expose the threads themselves.

What kind of Holocaust memorial would you build?

I don't know if there is a God, but I do believe in humanity. My faith has neither a Christ, nor a gospel. It has, however, an opposite. The opposite of what I believe is the Holocaust.

One can perhaps worship an antithesis in the service of one's faith more effectively than one can a divinity. The Holocaust is a negative image of my belief and this image has been deeply stamped on the world. In the depths of its impression I see the inverted spires of my faith. As I look into the deepest fissures I can imagine pulling them inside out:

* If the Holocaust concentrated Jews, homosexuals, the Roma, and all the other elements of German society who rendered it heterogeneous, and did

this so they could be murdered—very well: in my faith societies are alive only if they are mixed until the abolition of majority.

* If the Holocaust attempted to destroy the mentally ill, the physically disabled, the miscegenated and other embarrassments to racial purity—very well: in my faith difference ennobles.

* If the Holocaust slaughtered communists and the enemies of exploitation—very well: in my faith the advantages of wealth are no more than a heritable debt that holds one's humanity in hock until it is paid.

* If the Holocaust exploited bureaucracy's talent for walking guilt out of focus, until even the most ordinary person could perform mass murder—very well: in my faith any order I execute, I execute as though on my own children.

Memorials, statues, arches, headstones, time capsules all share the same difficulty. Theirs is a problem that makes them offensive and dangerous to any remembrance of the Holocaust.

For memorials to memorialize they must strip the flesh from whatever they're meant to commemorate and reupholster their subject in a material that can be exposed to history. This is how you go from George Washington the venal, jungle-fevering founding father to a 555 foot tall marble cock.

Memorials are first and always expensive machines made to flatten the lived experience of a person or event into an image. An image whose meaning is liquid and easily decanted into those who gaze upon it. This means memorials nearly never express what they were built to remember. Memorials tend instead to be excellent snapshots of a society in the act of flattering itself.

The Holocaust, then, is not a thing that should be memorialized. For if we stripped the memorious flesh from this event we would simply add another death to the total. The moment we allow an event to be memorialized is the same moment we have pressed that event into a capsule of irrelevance, as we do when a book has been closed and placed back on its shelf. And *everything* is lost in the gap between "remembered" and "reminded."

So I wouldn't build one. If you want a memorial you should build one for us, one that stands as a needle indicating the state of our memory. Do this instead of building one that kills for good what it was meant to preserve.

I would dig a trench in the middle of a city, clean across a city block. I'd line the trench with concrete and build ramps at either end. I would put a pile of cut diamonds in the center of the trench stretching from wall to wall and blocking your path as you walked along it. I would pour them into a cone three feet high. I'd light the trench but put no special lighting on the gems. The crowds in the narrow trench, as they jostle and shove to see the diamonds, would be intentional.

The inevitable thefts and the pile's diminishment would be the barometer of our memory. The sand running out of the glass, marking how much time until the next time. There would come a day when someone could walk from one end of the trench to the other without hearing the stones crunch beneath their feet, and that would be that.

Is NASA important?

Imagine you are lifted out of your house through a window. Your body rises above the roof and soon the outlines of your neighborhood come into view. You begin to recognize where you live from satellite images you've seen. Maybe you figure out which way is North. Everything assumes the miniature quality of the view out an airplane's window as it ascends after takeoff. You can see most of your city. Rising further, you see the horizon buckle into a shallow curve. The sky turns black, the Sun becomes a blinding cone of white light. You are in space. The Earth resolves into a ball and its continents are cocked to one side in an unfamiliar way. The Earth gets smaller and smaller. The last feature you can distinguish is an ice cap.

You are rising above the disc of the Solar System. On your right is a radiant expanse that hides the Sun. On your left are two or three points of light. Beneath your feet the Earth bleaches as it grows smaller. Soon it is a point of light that is impossible to distinguish from the other planets. The entire Solar System is at your feet. If you extend your right hand to cover the Sun and cast your face into shadow, every planet comes into view. Beyond and beneath the planets is a sparse silver sand of stars. The world is no longer everywhere but only straight down. As near as makes no difference, every book in the Universe is at exactly the same distance from you.

Space relieves us all in an objectively infinite way. The size of the Universe is its own absolution.

How do I stop wasting being 17?

The only way it is possible to waste being seventeen is to wish that you were eighteen.

When you're very young the world is full of atmospheres rather than objects. Think about what memories of childhood are like. They're memories of how things *felt*, not records of what happened. The red and white dimples that carpet pile presses into your bare knees. How burps smell after you've accidentally swallowed pool water. The static electricity that hisses and ticks as you drag your finger across the screen of a television tube. These grains of experience evaporate into the aura of what it was like to be a kid.

Then you get older. The cloud you lived in as a kid

starts to fall as sleet. Think about how the act of picking a movie changes. When you're seven the aura and excitement of *watching a movie* creeps like a fog into the act of picking one out and it almost doesn't matter which you choose. Ten years later you're weighing this film against that film, comparing tenths of an IMDb star, noticing how Lindsay Lohan doesn't look like a scuffed Barbie in it, and so on.

Life starts to turn dry. The grains of experience no longer evaporate. Instead they collect into little drifts. Lots of people get stuck here. For them the drifts turn into dunes and the dunes turn their lives into a desert of happenstance. These are the people who need a form to give their life a shape. The same way you pack beach sand into a bucket and flip it over to turn out a sandcastle's turret. (It goes without saying that this is what's happening when you get excited after you've bought something.) The point is that growing up is all too often growth in the wrong direction.

But which other way is there?

About two years before he died, Ludwig Wittgenstein was talking to somebody who asked him how he could admire a person like (Cardinal) John Henry

Newman. Newman believed in miracles, specifically the miracle of Napoleon's defeat at Moscow because the Pope had excommunicated him three years earlier. Anyways, Wittgenstein's response is your answer—

Wittgenstein: Twenty years ago I would have regarded Newman's action as incomprehensible, perhaps even insincere. But no more...

Somebody: But what changed in you that you no longer think so?

[silence]

W.: I came gradually to see that life is not what it seems.

[very long silence]

W.: It's like this: In the city, streets are nicely laid out. And you drive on the right and you have traffic lights, and so on. There are rules. When you leave the city, there are still roads, but no traffic lights. And when you get far off, there are no roads, no lights, no rules, nothing to guide you. It's all woods. And when you return to the city you may feel that the rules are wrong, that there should be no rules.

S.: I still don't understand.

   [silence]

W.: It comes to something like this—If you have a light, I say: Follow it. It may be right. Certainly life in the city won't do.

What do you think of the David Foster Wallace movie they made?

Many people don't know J.G.Ballard trained as a physician. There's an early short story of his called *The Drowned Giant*. It was written shortly after his wife died while on vacation with her family, of a pneumonia that doctors were unable to cure. In this story a 300 foot man washes up on the beach of an English resort town. 1964 was a fulcrum year. Ballard was disgusted by the medical profession and by himself. While his wife lived Ballard was bolted into a happiness that made his writing shallow. Her death thrust his three children on him in a way that made his compartment of self-satisfaction much too crowded any longer to soothe. After his wife's death Ballard was thrown back on himself, where he nearly foundered.

The town's inhabitants are awed at first by the presence of a man the size of a cathedral. They are timid about approaching his corpse on the tidal flat. But the giant quite naturally becomes an object of tourism, and even of affection. Children dare one another to climb over his face, to leap across the black well of his parted lips and curl up in the orbits of his cloudy eyes. Then, as the man begins to putrefy, his flesh is stripped from his bones and sold to factories for cat food and fertilizer. His penis is dug out by the root on the orders of a theatrical promoter. The promoter has it skinned, dried, and loaded onto a truck where it follows a traveling circus, misadvertised as the member of a whale.

Whether you like it or not, whether you're a fan or not, whether you're tending some memorial flame or embroidering the edge of a disintegrating memory, whether you're canning his posterity or wrapping death in chintz by referring to his suicide with despicable platitudes, if your connection to David Foster Wallace is personal *in any way* you will find yourself in the crowd that gathered on the beach in Ballard's story. You are by turns deluded, callous, ghoulish, given to flabby eulogy, aroused by profit, paralyzed by glory, or worst of all, drunk on intimacy.

The giant is dead, and though we will continue to gather around it to suck meaning from the corpse (we are helpless to do anything else), we will find that the flesh—flesh of the body or flesh of the spirit—can be sliced only so thin before its sections surrender to transparency and finally, nothingness.

And in the end, when only the ribs at low tide remain, when every exploitation has been undertaken and every last bubble of fruitless intimacy blown and burst, there will be what there always was—what there has always been in the face of death—the story.

Is physical beauty important?

On April 14th, 1919 the sister of Marcel Duchamp, Suzanne, married one of his closest friends,
the painter Jean Crotti. Marcel's wedding present to
the couple arrived by mail three weeks later. It was a
letter that contained a set of instructions for a work
of art his sister and brother-in-law were to make.
His letter said to take a geometry textbook, to open
it, and then to bind it with wire to the metal railing
of their apartment's balcony. It was to be left out in
the weather until it learned the facts of life.

That's you and all of us. We have ideas about
beauty, axioms that describe how faces ought to
look and even rules for the right texture of skin. But
right now, as you're reading this, rays from space are

entering your body and destroying the elasticity of the collagen in your skin. With every smile, with every expression of disapproval, you are stretching proteins that, thanks to this cosmic barrage, will no longer return your skin to its original and attractive tension. Wrinkles come from emotion and the particles shed by dying stars.

Beauty is a game that does not permit those who can compete to retire as champions. What do you do when you're faced with a game that no one can win but which everyone feels compelled to play? What's the point of squeezing yourself for the rest of your life in order to contribute your several drops to the ocean of human knowledge? Or culture? Duchamp was in Buenos Aires when his sister was married and he wrote a letter about how any game a person felt compelled to play was also a game whose rules anyone could change.

What does entering a profession mean to you?

A profession is only one in a series of concentric shells that enclose you in an ordered whole. Each shell is opaque and their opacity inclines us to think its surface the ultimate horizon of our lives. The penetration of each shell as you proceed outward, and away from your self, is felt as a realization. To remain trapped within a particular shell betrays a special sort of small-minded obstinacy.

Two good examples of this are fossil fuels and Adolf Eichmann.

Around two billion years ago elementary life developed that was able to use metal ions like vanadium or magnesium to catalyze the destruction of water molecules when sunlight shone on them. This process, later called photosynthesis, produced oxygen gas and energized hydrogen nuclei. The energy contained in the hydrogen was used in turn to crack open molecules of carbon dioxide, making them available for the assembly of complicated organic compounds. Which in turn composed cellular life. The oxygen was of no further use to the organisms whose photosynthesis had produced it and the gas simply dissolved away into the ancient oceans.

For something like two hundred million years this oxygen reacted with chemicals in the ocean and with rocks on the Earth's surface, binding to them and becoming trapped. By this process it was prevented from contributing to the atmosphere's oxygen content, which—at this point in Earth's history—was essentially zero. But in the end these chemical sinks became saturated and free oxygen began for the first time to accumulate in the atmosphere.

Within about fifty million years the oxygen content of Earth's atmosphere and oceans had risen to levels that poisoned much of the life then living. This extinction had the effect of favoring the photosynthetic organisms that had perpetrated it and thereby awarded to them a much larger share of the Earth's resources.

These were the organisms whose success accounts for the existence of petroleum and coal today.

By about 360 million years ago these photosynthesizing organisms had raised the free-oxygen level far beyond its present-day value to something over a third of the planet's atmosphere. This enormous supply of oxygen permitted the evolution and success of multicellular animals, whose biology rotated around the respiration of this gas into chemical energy. Hence, us.

At the same time the success of these algae and early plants was such that the dead body of one would frequently be buried beneath the living body of another too quickly for the dead one to rot. Over several million years these mats of preserved tissue became encased in layers of sedimentary rocks. The heat and pressure these rocks exerted began to break down the complicated chemical architectures so painstakingly assembled by photosynthesis. Depending upon geological vagaries, this degradation produced seams of coal, veins of oil, pockets of natural gas, or mixtures of all three. Which we then mined and burnt for fuel.

At this point one of those concentric shells obstructs our understanding of what we're doing when we press the gas pedal with our foot, read a book, eat an apple, or do literally anything at all.

It isn't that we fail to understand all these activities as dependent upon fossil fuels (the gasoline is obvious, the black ink in which the words of the book are printed is oil-based, the wax that protected the apple during its cold-storage is distilled from petroleum.) Rather, we fail to see that by using fossil fuels in this way we are participating in an enormous reversal of the photosynthetic activity responsible for creating them in the first place.

I mean this literally. Photosynthesis destroys a water molecule to create free oxygen and two hydrogen atoms later used to trap carbon dioxide in a complicated organic compound. Burning fossil fuels (and burning only accomplishes all-at-once what making plastics or waxes or ink from oil succeeds in doing piecemeal) destroys free oxygen and an organic compound to create molecules of water and carbon dioxide. The entirety of modern society is founded on performing photosynthesis in reverse. To create, among other things, light. (And not just any light. We prefer ours to be as close to the color of sunlight as possible, and have elaborately designed our sources of artificial illumination to produce the very same yellow that lit the first photosynthetic cells.)

The point here is not that chemistry can teach us the deep history of apple waxes. The point is the way in which available energy on this planet—and life itself—oscillates between abundance and scarcity depending on the existence of an effective catalyst. Before a magnesium ion became trapped in the center of a chlorophyll molecule, life on Earth was indifferent to sunlight and unfamiliar with free oxygen. After this catalytic breakthrough sunlight was converted into enough free oxygen to exterminate 90% of all species then living on Earth. Permitting photosynthetic organisms to inherit the Earth after poisoning it. Before the development of human cleverness, the posthumous existence of these organisms was irrelevant to the animals whose respiration photosynthesis made possible. But after it, *after* human cleverness catalyzed first the extraction of this ancient energy and then its return to water and carbon dioxide—well, it's already called the Quaternary extinction. Not that anything intelligent enough to need a name appears likely to survive it.

As life and death sweep across the face of this planet you realize that success and failure are embedded within one another. That is what it feels like to pierce one of these shells. To see a horizon become larger the further you get from self-centeredness. Eichmann is a counterexample.

Eichmann was a consummate professional. This means that he was, both by temperament and choice, comfortable living and working within a narrow horizon. He was an excellent example of the kind of person who remains indifferent to their captivity within a concentric nest of shells. He was selfish and self-serving. He frequently billed his office for the lavish parties he loved to throw and was shameless about flattering his superiors. But more than any unsavory personal attribute or explicit cruelty, Eichmann was the opposite of good because of his inability to think. Hannah Arendt depicts him as almost totally unable to perceive what somebody else's point of view might contain. His self-centeredness made him incapable of reaching out to grasp that which did not originate within him, and this species of deep stupidity rendered him capable of bureaucratizing genocide. It is not a coincidence that he is described as having read only one or two serious books in his life.

Consequences are often difficult to predict. First, sunlight begins to oxygenate the ancient Earth, which sets in motion one extinction and then, two billion years later, a middle manager is allocating coal and natural gas so locomotives and ovens can facilitate another. An extinction that converted undesirable persons and free oxygen into carbon dioxide and ash.

In this world anyone who wants to make their life *about* something is trying to get from A to Z. From the elementary to the subtle. The form this progress will take is frequently unclear, but the line along which each of your realizations will eventually lie radiates—always and only—away from a selfish heart.

Aren't we all just meat?

Writing in 1757, Abbé Nicolas Trublet says that

In 1695 the writer Bernard de Fontenelle visited the radical Cartesian priest Nicolas Malebranche in Paris, at his home in the Oration abbey on the rue Saint-Honoré. Fontenelle later told me that

A very pregnant household dog entered the hall in which Father Malebranche and I were walking. The dog came up to Father Malebranche, licked his hand, lay down, and rolled over at his feet. Malebranche made several gestures to drive the dog away, but these were in vain. Suddenly, Malebranche gave the dog a enormous kick, which drew from her a scream of pain and from myself a cry of compassion.

What?

said Malebranche icily,

Don't you know that this thing didn't feel it?

How do you break addictions?

recall the Marina Abramović bit where she locked
lips with a partner and they breathed each other's
breaths until one of them passed out

now recall how we stand in precisely the same relationship to trees—speeding, as we do, though a vacu-
um on our island lung

but, far from killing one another, our respective ex-
halations are just what the other needs to respire

or again, Big Jim Hogg, the twentieth governor of
Texas, whose enormous body—as stipulated in his
will—was buried beneath a pecan tree rather than a
headstone

and the pecans that fell from the tree, which were

gathered and planted the length and breadth of the state

the body being after all only a skein of yarn, filamentary, and by its nature having a beginning and an end

but this slavery to a single dimension disappears once you've begun to knit, and felt yourself join a general fabric

and *fear of being* becomes dissolved in the higher surfaces

How do you choose a person to spend your entire life with?

George Eliot's *Middlemarch* contains one of the most frightening passages in literature. Eliot (who did the equivalent of doctoral study on Spinoza) is trying to write what it's like to be a mind in the world. She describes the concave steel mirrors that used to be placed behind candle flames to magnify their light. These mirrors would easily tarnish and needed to be polished frequently. This polishing tended to make tiny, random, and densely crisscrossed scratches on the surface of the steel. When the mirror was fitted to the candlestick however, the light of the flame picked out only those scratches that happened to create concentric circles.

Eliot says that the flame is you and that the illusion of concentric scratches is what happens to that you when it goes out into the world.

Everyone's had this realization, usually when looking down on a city from the window of a tall building: 'Holy shit! All those people have their own lives and every one of them is going well or badly and each life seems just as important to each person as mine does to me.' But her point is not really about our egotism and its tendency to stunt an interest in the lives of others. Her point is about the people who are the opposite of strangers. The terror bubbles up when you realize it's precisely the people to whom we are the closest that are most strongly distorted by the self. In this way, the people whom we love the most are transformed into golems of the mind's own silt: You can imagine the minds of most people as a column of flame on which are focused the gazes of concentric ranks of creatures risen from this.

Our talent for instantaneously rendering the world into monsters who speak only what we would prefer to hear is one of love's greatest dangers. There is a fatal tendency to fall in love with people who are nothing to you except their adoration of your best-loved qualities. This is what you call falling in love when it's a solution to the problem of being a self. These are the people who secretly look at their own reflection and at nothing deeper when they look into the eyes of the person with whom they're exchanging vows. Loneliness dines on this gaze.

If you dive away from the thoroughly empty symbolism of marriage and peer deep inside the wedding ring, it's possible to see a way out of this nightmare.

Metals are metals because of sharing. Metals are ductile, conductors of heat and electricity, by turns flexible or malleable or springy because of how they share electrons. Imagine you're inside that ring and standing on the surface of an atomic nucleus. The space above you is filled with electrons. Those closer to you tend to orbit, but beyond these there is an ocean in the sky. The farthest electrons are shared. These wander throughout the ring. They belong to no atom but they are the source of every trait the ring possesses. They fill the voids between the atoms of gold like the water in a pool and it is these who slosh back and forth when an electric current is applied. They were the lubricant that allowed the atoms to slide past one another when the jeweler sized the ring. It was this ocean of electrons that kept the molten gold from evaporating when the ring was cast. These traits do not emerge from some solid self, do not come from some permanent identity but rather from the communal flow of particles that are the property of no one.

You are your corporeal self, just as the nucleus beneath your feet has a quantity of protons and neutrons—the numbers of which assign it a fixed identity on the periodic table—but everything else about that metal, about you, about me, has been an emanation of flow.

It's time to spend the rest of your life with someone when you are no particular either in a community of two.

Did you see the new Mad Max?

When I was a kid I was always fantasizing about getting sick. Sickness, profound sickness, had the same beckoning, hypnotic effect on me as the edge of a cliff. A girl in my school had a trisomy disorder. It grew worse before my eyes until she was pulled out of our class. She'd be talking about safari animals or *The Simpsons* and then her head would slowly pivot up and off to one side, as though she were pausing to think. And then she'd just be off somewhere very else. The most frightening thing was how her hands changed. Over the course of the school year her middle fingers would creep across her forefingers in an involuntary gesture of luck. Eventually these fingers couldn't be uncrossed and she became unable to write. Crossed fingers have seemed to invite catastrophe to me ever since.

The other sickness that haunted me as a child was fatal familial insomnia. This is a vanishingly rare condition in which a person slowly loses the ability to sleep. At first they simply can't sleep through the night. This makes them irritable, as it would anyone. But then, as their insomnia worsens, layer after layer of their humanity is peeled away. Irritability gives way to intense phobias about things that had previously seemed innocuous. These phobias generate intense panic attacks, paranoias, and eventually outright psychosis. As their ability to sleep is steadily destroyed over the next several months the person hallucinates almost continually. Finally they are unable to sleep at all. This is the terminal stage. They stop eating, begin steadily losing weight, become unresponsive both to communication and to pain. And then, after six or eight months of perfect wakefulness, they die.

It made me think of scurvy or rickets, diseases that showcase all the ways in which a vitamin—whose presence we take for granted—can destroy life when absent. Fatal familial insomnia is a vile experiment that nature performs to demonstrate that sleep and dreaming are as essential to life as vitamins C or D.

I fantasized about insomnia grating away my mind. Looking back, I think I was entranced by the necessity of the immaterial to life. That's how I explain my dark attraction to this hideous way of dying. It's relatively easy to understand how vitamins facilitate the hundreds of thousands of distinct chemical reactions that produce biological life; less easy to understand how sleep, and the dreams which flourish in it, permit us to *know* we are alive.

I began to think of a hierarchy—

1. Nutrients like vitamins or sugar that enable the sort of life which molecular biology studies
2. 'Nutrients' like sleep and dreaming that enable the sort of life which psychology studies
3. ?

Does something happen in waking life analogous to these? Something to enable a sort of life that sits atop the other two? I started to think waking life also has its dreams and that these nurture a further sort of life. This further sort of life, I realized, is the one that lives in stories.

Stories, with their paths of necessity and engines of plot are the dreams we dream while awake. I thought of them as 'dreams' because these daylight fantasies nurture our waking life just as those we have in sleep protect our minds. It's easy to dismiss this, but then again—imagine a hair cell on your head, living its life, pushing out its follicle. And even if it's an inch away from the physical site of your dreams, what does it know about them?

The dreams of sleep are solitary and the waking consciousness they permit is tragically individual. But the dreams that stories permit are communal. Public dreaming.

Imagine an alien who does not sleep. What could be stranger than watching all of humanity go into a dark room every night and become inert for a third of each day? Likewise—to an alien who could not experience our communal dreaming in stories— what could be more incomprehensible than *billions* of people, each apparently individual, gathering in enormous, darkened rooms, calmly sitting side by side, and watching a dream projected on one wall?

'Humanity' exists because of this community of dreamers.

Joseph Campbell spent most of his life trying to find the eternal recurrences in our communal dreams and to anyone with eyes *Mad Max* is a movie made in total consciousness of this fact. The movie is a cathedral consecrated to the greater glory of the monomyth. No one needs me to point out all the ways this is true, nor how every idea in every frame has been boiled down to the mythological equivalent of an essential oil.

But think about the moment, early on, when Max is strapped to the hood of Nick Hoult's Chevrolet: Max is pumping blood through an IV line that has been woven through the links of a chain, a chain that connects the two men and by which one gives blood to the other. This image makes plain what's true for all of us but which *individuals* cannot see. One can wander, but two are always going somewhere. We're all of us linked by the umbilical of dreams.

Is nigger a bad word?

My only thought about this is that the word cannot be separated from the mouth that pronounces it.

White people who insist on being able to use the word because black people 'can' are really just white people demanding a black person extend precisely the terms of equality which the white world has scrupulously denied black people.

And this is the particle of arrogance that, when set alongside every other white person whose thoughts move in the same pattern, assumes the shape and weight of white supremacy.

Who makes race real?

This makes me think of something that happened last night. I was walking at about eight o'clock. The sky was overcast and the light bouncing between the Earth and the clouds gave it a purple color. Above me were thousands and thousands of crows. For as long as I can remember, and probably for hundreds of years before, enormous flocks of crows have flown over this spot every evening.

The crows were flying into a headwind and remained almost stationary above me. The flock seemed to shimmer. One crow would bank its wings in a way that caught more wind than the others' and this motion made it catch more light. The crows around it followed suit. This change happened in a rippling, radial way that made me think of a still pond disturbed; as though there were, high above me, a surface of crows and this surface were being disturbed by invisible drops from a source higher still. I tried to take a video with my phone. This didn't work. The crows seemed much further away on the screen. Their shimmering was completely lost. I was disappointed and I began to wonder why.

It occurred to me that my phone's failure to capture what I saw was one end of a very long thread. The phone's camera saw the sky as a grid. Each square in this grid had two possible states: light or dark. This restriction caused the camera's failure to see what I did. The numerous crows, the subtle effect of the light on their wings, the delicate balance between individual birds and the unified effect their motion created, all of this revealed a weakness of seeing the world through a binary grid. This weakness is caused by a philosophical division of the world into 'there' and 'not there.' This division was then encoded into the architecture of the computer that assembled my unsatisfying video. It's a division which has been latent in Western thought for two and a half thousand years. And the weakness of this way of thinking was suddenly clear when I tried to record the crows behaving as more than individuals.

It might seem silly to indict Western thought because I tried to record crows with a cellphone from a hundred feet away. A sensible person might say 'Get closer' or 'Use a real camera and a tighter lens.' These suggestions are solutions to the problem of seeing the crows more clearly. But helpful as they are, they do not address the fact that a problem was possible in the first place. Further, one of the best ways of seeing straight to the heart of something is to find its ragged edges. It is precisely where systems of thought begin to fray that the possibility of transcending them seems most obvious. You ought to be suspicious, for similar reasons, when someone tries to correct your mistake by pointing you in the direction of a system's sweet spot. If you lose your keys under a broken streetlight the solution is not to look beneath a working one. You must bring your own light.

Racists are often most racist when they attempt to help those they oppress. This is because—like anyone trapped inside an inadequate system of thought—racists tend to imagine the difficulties of others as a kind of ignorance (just as my difficulty in filming the crows was seen as a type of ignorance by the person suggesting solutions.) For this reason racists frequently direct those they oppress into tighter and tighter relationships with racism. Here's Lyndon Johnson doing it:

> [T]here was an incident that occurred one morning in Johnson's limousine while [Robert] Parker was driving him from his Thirtieth Place house to the Capitol. Johnson, who had been reading a newspaper in the back seat, "suddenly ... lowered the newspaper and leaned forward," and said, " 'Chief, does it bother you when people don't call you by name?' "
>
> Parker was to recall that "I answered cautiously but honestly, 'Well, sir, I do wonder. My name is Robert Parker.' " And that was evidently not an answer acceptable to Johnson. "Johnson slammed the paper onto the seat as if he was slapping my face. He leaned close to my ear. 'Let me tell you one thing, nigger,' he shouted. 'As long as you are black, and you're gonna be black till the day you die, no one's gonna call you by your goddamn name. So no matter what you are called, nigger, you just let it roll off your back like water, and you'll make

it. Just pretend like you're a goddamn piece of furniture.' "

Parker introduces himself by name and makes the first motion towards a friendship. Johnson immediately tells Parker "You are alone and must act it at all times. Then racism won't matter to you anymore." And if ever racism had a wheelhouse, a central point of maximum effectiveness, it lies in isolating the oppressed and telling them their oppression is meaningless. Know a system by its denial of the possibility of life beyond it.

Despite the fact that a system like racism can seem, to a racist, to stretch from horizon to horizon, it is not the same as reality. Racism is real, but only in the sense that a megalomaniacal thread might claim to be the tapestry. Reality is much more like a fabric—permeable and multicolored—than any of the systems which compose its patchwork would have you believe.

Who knows where that conversation in the limousine might have gone if Johnson had said "It's nice to meet you Robert, I'm Lyndon." Who knows what the world would look like if our technology were premised on something other than black-and-white thinking? Mistakes in tapestries must be unthreaded at the fringe. And there too, new patterns can be woven, but by our own light.

How could they acquit George Zimmerman?

It's very easy to feel defeated when the false becomes true.

You can think of the Law as an enormous simulation of the world, one in which everything has been accounted for by some legal approximation (for example, land becomes 'property'.) Questions are fed into it, hands turn the crank, and out comes 'what happened,' according to Law. This is why bad verdicts hurt so much: they are given the force of truth because each of us has no choice but to live under the gaze of the Law and within its grasp. The Law recognizes no one who declines categorization within it.

Legislations are general truths that have been enacted inside this system ("The life of a human person cannot be taken without a compelling reason," etc.) Verdicts are the further, particular truths deduced from these ("The defendant killed for a sufficiently compelling reason.") Laws against murder erect a set of truths about human life and murder verdicts establish the truth about particular acts that caused a person's death. Laws define reality inside this legal simulation of the world and verdicts compute the truths that populate it. Every single one of us has—from the moment of our conception—lived inside this simulation and been shaped by what it deems true. The Law is the most powerful machine we use to manufacture our reality.

George Zimmerman's defense attorney placed a large piece of concrete before the jury box during his closing arguments and, referring to it, said:

> That is cement, that is a sidewalk, and that is not an unarmed teen carrying nothing but Skittles, trying to get home.

He went on to say that Trayvon Martin used the "availability" of the sidewalk on which he was standing as a weapon against George Zimmerman.

However powerful the Law may seem when it shapes our reality, it remains a machine. And when you feed it heinous trash like Stand Your Ground, when you eliminate the requirement to flee before using deadly force, the Law is very much garbage in, garbage out. If you decide reality features the right to kill to soothe one's own anxiety then the machine will diligently compute the disgusting absurdity that a teenager is armed if he has access to a sidewalk. The Law will say—speaking from the throne of its majesty—that the only truly innocent posture a person can adopt is that of being unmoored from gravity, bobbing helplessly in space. These disgusting absurdities have now been given the force of truth. This is dangerous because truth—as featured in the reality Law creates—does not convince or persuade. The truth is far too powerful. Rather, truth creates the kind of person required to believe it.

This recently computed truth will create two kinds of people. First, it will needlessly duplicate George Zimmerman into a legion of armed cowards and second, it will add enormously to another class of people: victims. Some members of this second group will be subject to the physical predation of the first. But all of them will have been victims of a far more tragic kind of violence. They will be the kind of people who cannot imagine an escape from the reality this legal truth has created. The kind of people for whom injustice is woven into the physical matter where they stand and on which the law of gravity compels them to remain.

The most important freedom it is possible for a human to experience will be denied to this type of person: This is the freedom to crawl towards the wall separating our legal simulation of reality from the wilderness it was created to exclude, the freedom to see beyond it and glimpse there the indigenous truths. Truths whose beauty is so frequently destroyed when they are captured and bent toward society's interest.

How do you explain the new kind of Civil Rights Movement that is happening right now with #blacklivesmatter?

It isn't a new kind of anything. It fits into the template of nonviolent resistance. This time, however, there is a sickening twist.

I'll tell you a story:

Gandhi was probably the first person to realize a war for independence could be won in newspapers instead of on battlefields. That is, Gandhi realized that if you could show the body of imperialism what the hands had to do in order to feed it then that body would recoil in a spasm of self-consciousness.

To this end Gandhi led peaceful protestors into the brutality and murder by which British colonialism sustained itself in India. He did this on such a scale and with so single-minded a purpose that it was covered by Western journalism. The reporting that carried this violence from the extremity of the British Empire into its heartland held a mirror up to the ogre's face. And India—which had not been conquered on the order of some popular referendum of Englishmen but instead by the rapacity and avarice of the British aristocracy—came to be seen for what it was: a victim of one of the greatest feats of greed ever carried out.

On April 9th, 1950 Martin Luther King, Jr. heard a black preacher named Mordecai Johnson (then the president of Howard University) speak in Philadelphia. Johnson had spent some time in India and spoke at length about the philosophical underpinnings of Gandhi's method.

To Gandhi, nonviolence was a matchless weapon. This is because it is founded on a concept called *satyagraha*. In Sanskrit this word means something like 'truth-force' or 'the persuasive power of love.' Nonviolent resistance could never be defeated because it was founded on love for one's enemies. This love is the source of a protester's refusal to attack his or her adversary with physical violence. In Gandhi's hands, and with the help of the international press, this weapon had just been used to win the independence of 390 million people.

King later said that this talk was so "electrifying that I left the meeting and went out and purchased half a dozen books on Gandhi's life and works." King was then still a student at Crozer Theological Seminary, just south of Philadelphia. That Sunday in 1950 was the beginning of nonviolent resistance in the American Civil Rights movement.

In reading about Gandhi's philosophy and the strategy for Indian independence that it generated, Martin Luther King came to several realizations:

Nonviolent resistance refuses to participate in evil, but not in the same way that pacifism refuses. If pacifism simply refuses to participate in evil, nonviolent resistance is a passionate and relentless intervention in the lives of those who *do* participate in evil. In this way, King saw that the basic tension in any racial struggle was not *between* the races but instead *within in the hearts* of those who oppress. A tension between the basic desire of all human beings to be good and the racist conditioning by which life in America blunts this desire and bends their actions, instead, toward evil. King, like Gandhi before him, realized nonviolent resistance was a way of untwisting the hearts of those bent upon doing evil. Both men saw nonviolent resistance as a kind of therapy the oppressed performed on the oppressor. Imagine—

1. The unarmed crowd approaches the line of colonial police.
2. The police draw their clubs and by their violent intent reveal the evil in their hearts.
3. The unarmed crowd is beaten bloody.
4. And in the pools of spilled blood the oppressors see themselves reflected, not as they are told they are, but as they really are.
5. And this realization is carried to the four corners of the Earth by the journalists whom Gandhi invited to observe.

Nonviolent resistance works by forcing the oppressor—whether he is a single colonial policeman or the most distant beneficiary of the British Empire—to see themselves as they really are.

King realized the American heart had been similarly twisted and American society rendered ignorant of itself as a result. American society thought itself good but night after night found itself throwing ropes over the branches of pecan trees, found itself refusing to see the oppression and savagery by which it had come to be, found itself in a three-hundred-and-fifty-year moral sleepwalk. King realized American society could be brought to self-consciousness, could finally *find itself*, by forcing the evil at its heart into broad daylight while television cameras observed.

In this sense King's project of national therapy was the opposite of Black Power. King sought to absolve every white heart with black blood. Malcolm X would have happily left America to stew in its richly deserved national guilt so long as black bodies were immune to attack. It's not hard to feel Malcolm's rage and it was not easy for King to explain himself to the militant wing of black liberation. It is difficult to claim that the black answer to three hundred and fifty years of exploitation, rape, and murder should be a willingness—and even a *duty*—to have your jaw broken by a riot police.

In the end both leaders were assassinated. The Civil Rights Movement hit its high water mark and ran its course, without Martin Luther King or

Malcolm X. And America settled into forty years of self-satisfied eulogy for one of them, backsliding all the while.

We are now in the middle of a new campaign of nonviolent resistance. This campaign has no leader, no organizing committee, no controls, no *satyagraha*, and no participants except the police and their victims.

Oscar Grant, Aiyana Jones, Tamir Rice, Walter Scott, Ezell Ford, Marlene Pinnock, Eric Garner, Sam DuBose, Laquan McDonald, Alton Sterling, Philando Castille—and every other person whose death and brutalization was captured by a camera for all to see—are these participants. Each has been unwillingly drafted into a national demonstration of the contempt with which black bodies can be treated in America. The ubiquitous presence of cameras has done this. These cameras record the nonviolence of black people and the lethal force with which this is met by police.

Black life in America is lived so wholly on the edge of a knife that the most trivial interaction between a black person and the police has mortal consequences. Videos of these mortal consequences are drilling into the twisted American heart just as the televised brutality of Birmingham did in 1963. The manifest innocence and nonviolence of those brutalized and killed by police on camera are forcing the American heart to face itself, again.

And though this new campaign drills into the same old heart and sparks the same self-consciousness Martin Luther King sought to kindle there, it bears a critical difference from hierarchical campaigns for civil rights. The new campaign is *emergent*: It is generated by the friction of circumstance and not the labor of an organization. *This means the present campaign of nonviolent resistance cannot be stopped.*

Martin Luther King could be shot and America could fall asleep when he ceased to breathe, but these police murders will continue to occur as a *matter of circumstance* and as *matters of circumstance* they will continue to be recorded by cameras.

Whatever activism is bred on the outrage, or handwringing, or excuses these recordings produce, this activism will be secondary to the *campaign*. The campaign and its draft of circumstance will continue to select innocent and unresisting black people to join in death those whose murders have been recorded. This is quite unlike the extraordinary situations Gandhi and Martin Luther King created, the situations by which the oppressor was forced to see his own face, forced to feel the evil in his own heart when his police beat defenseless crowds.

The new campaign has not been created because the new campaign, like racism itself, is happening everywhere and at all times. And from this angle, America is now a society that can no longer avoid the mirror.

I want to give up.

A while ago we were in New York City, at the back of an Indian restaurant. This was one of six on the same block in the West Village, the set of six everyone knew were serviced by an enormous common kitchen deep underground and linked to the storefronts by semi-legal tunnels. The three of us sat by the flapping door to this restaurant's kitchen-tunnel. The door had red vinyl upholstery and let out clouds of steam or the sound of distant screaming when a waiter pushed through it. One of my friends was talking to the other, who was a classical pianist. They were speaking well above my head until my friend casually asked her how she had come to her staccato delivery. She laughed, looked at the ceiling for a moment, and said this it was a story in itself.

She'd had a breakdown midway through her conservatory training. She knew she had talent, even more talent than is normal at conservatories, but nevertheless had felt, one day, that her playing had hit a wall. The point of playing, she explained, was to unroll and press into her own chest the suite of emotions the composer felt. Once these were there—burning inside of her—she could play the piece as it was meant to be heard. Her problem was not feeling what the composer felt. She said her problem was in her hands. She had been taught a smooth and flowing style of performance and her hands had so completely absorbed this lesson that she found it impossible to play in any other way. Try as she might and no matter how many hours she practiced, she simply became more technically proficient in, as she said, the wrong language.

She finally came to a crisis and decided to quit playing altogether. In despair, she went to her mentor at the conservatory, confessed her problem and her intention to leave the school. The mentor listened patiently. When she had finished, he dug a business card out from under the sheet of glass that covered his desk. "Go and see this woman," her mentor said. It was the business card of a Jungian therapist with an address in the West Village. Her mentor explained that the therapist specialized in musical complexes, and had a large circle of professional musicians among her clientele.

The woman listened to her story in a tiny office that smelled like cardamom. When the story was finished she told the pianist her problem was not psychological but only technical.

She told her to go home and to set up her ironing board. She should sit at it as though it were the console of a piano. She told her to turn on the iron, set it to high heat, and nestle it in a towel so its plate pointed up. Once it was hot, she should suck the tips of her fingers, and play the hot metal of the iron as though it were her piano's keys. She should listen to the hiss as her saliva became steam. She told her to try and control the duration of the hiss until it was as brief as possible. When the pianist was satisfied she had done this, she should continue to play the iron but without wetting her fingers. Pain, the therapist said, should be her only object of attention. How long could she keep her fingers pressed to the hot iron? The therapist said she must learn to play her pain as her fingertips pressed the hot metal. Then, she must imagine that each key on her piano were as hot as the plate on her iron. This must be her new way of understanding the piano. Playing must become difficult for her again. Only then would her style change.

She did what the therapist said and found it revolutionized her relationship to music. She said she no longer thought of herself as a pianist and that she had become an artist of difficulty instead.

List of Shibboleth Names by which the Privileged Judge Their Inferiors

A

Chinua Achebe, Nigerian novelist
(***chin**-oo-ah ah-**chay**-bae*)

Chimamanda Ngozi Adichie, Nigerian novelist
(*chim-ah-**man**-da nnnn-**go**-zeh ah-**dee**-che*)

James Agee, American novelist and screenwriter
(***a**-jee*)

Anna Akhmatova, dissident Soviet poet
(*onna ock-**mah**-taugh-vah*)

Louis Althusser, French Marxist philosopher
(*lou-**wee** **al**-too-sair*)

Jerzy Andrzejewski, Polish novelist
(***yer**-zhay ahn-zhay-**ev**-ski*)

Roger Angell, American baseball writer
(*angel*)

Jean Anouilh, French dramatist
(French pronunciation: ~***ahn**'oo-ee*)

Diane Arbus, American photographer
(*dee-**ann***)

Hannah Arendt, German philosopher
(***hahn**-ah **ahr**-ent*)

Martha Argerich, Argentine pianist
  (*mar-tah herr-each*)

Eugène Atget, French photographer
  (*oo-zhenne at-zhey*)

Augustine of Hippo, early Christian philosopher
  (*aw-gus-tin*)

Autechre, English electronic musicians
  (*aw-tekk-er*)

Richard Ayoade, English comedian and film director
  (*eye-oh-wah-dee*)

B

Angelo Badalamenti, American film composer
  (*bottle-ah-menti*)

Walter Bagehot, English journalist
  (*badget*)

Balliol College, Oxford University
  (*bay-lee-uhl*)

Donald/Frederick Barthelme, American
postmodern writer/minimalist writer
  (*barth-uhl-me*)

Karl Barth, Swiss Protestant theologian
(*bart*)

Roland Barthes, French literary theorist
(*bart*)

Tom Beauchamp, American philosopher
(*beachum*)

Walter Benjamin, German Marxist humanist
(***ben***-*yameen*)

John Berger, English art critic
(*berdger*)

Bishop Berkeley, Irish empiricist philosopher
(*barkley*)

Hans Bethe, German nuclear physicist
(*beta*)

John Betjeman, English poet
(***betch***-*uh-mun*)

Joseph Beuys, German Fluxus artist
(*boyz*)

Tadeusz Borowski, Polish writer and Holocaust
survivor
(*tah-**de**-yoosh borr-**off**-ski*)

Hieronymus Bosch, Flemish painter
(Flemish pronunciation: *heer-**rone**-nee-mohse boss*)

Anthony Boucher, American mystery writer
(rhymes with *voucher*)

Tycho Brahe, Danish astronomer
(Danish pronunciation: ***too**-ghoh brahhh*)

Broad Art Museum, Los Angeles
(*brode*)

Hermann Broch, Austrian modernist fiction writer
(*~**hair**-monn brohhh*)

Burgundy Street, New Orleans
(*burr-**gun**-dee*)

Steve Buscemi, American actor
(*boo-**semm**-ee*)

Bowdoin College, Brunswick, Maine
(***boh**-din*)

C

Gonville and Caius College, University of Cambridge
(*keys*)

Menzies Campbell, Scottish politician
(*ming-iss*)

Karel Čapek, Czech dramatist
(*kah-**rell chap**-eck*)

Robert Campin, Flemish painter
(***com**-pin*)

Thomas Carew, English Cavalier poet
(*carey*)

Vija Celmins, Latvian-American visual artist
(***vee**-yah **tell**-midge*)

Michael Chabon, American novelist
(***shay**-bonn*)

J.C. Chandor, American film director
(***shann**-door*)

Dan Chaon, American fiction writer
(*shawn*)

Chyron, broadcast news graphic technology
(***kai**-rawn* or ***kai**-run*)

Cimabue, Italian painter
(*chee-ma-**boo**-ee*)

Michael Cimino, American film director
   (*chee-**me**-noh*)

Emil Cioran, Romanian-French philosopher and pessimist
   (*chore-**ahn***)

Ta-Nehisi Coates, American journalist and memoirist
   (***tah**-nuh-**hah**-see*)

Alexander/Andrew/Patrick Cockburn,
   Irish journalists
   (*coburn*)

Paulo Coelho, Brazilian novelist
   (*~**pow**-lu kuh-**whey.l**-you.*)[1]

J.M. Coetzee, South African novelist
   (*koot-**see***)

William Cowper, English poet
   (*cooper*)

Cré na Cille, Máirtín Ó Cadhain book
   (*~kreh neh **kill**-eh*)

Mihaly Csikszentmihalyi, Hungarian psychologist
   (*me-**high cheek**-sent-me-high*)

---

1   Portuguese has a much more complicated phonetics than English
and so this is especially approximate.

Alfonso/Jonás/Carlos Cuarón,
Mexican film directors
(*al-fone-so/ho-nas kwah-roan*)

Countee Cullen, American poet
(*cown-tay*)

Marie Skłodowska-Curie, Polish-French chemist
(*skwoh-doaf-ska*)

Jan Czochralski, Polish chemist and metallurgist
(*yann choh-h'ral-ski*)

D

The Dalles, Oregon
(*the dolls*)

Gerard David, Flemish painter
(Flemish pronunciation: *~hhheer-ahrd dahh-fidd*)

Guy Debord, French Marxist theorist
(*ghee du-borrh*)

Louis De Broglie, French physicist
(*duh broy*)

Giorgio De Chirico, Italian painter
(Italian pronunciation: *~dee kee-ree-koh*)

Richard Dedekind, German mathematician
(between *day-dah-kin* and *day-dah-kint*)

Wilhelm Dilthey, German psychologist
(*dill-tai*)

Alfred Döblin, German novelist
(*deu-bleen*)

Don Juan, Byron character
(*jew-un*)

Gerrit/Gerard Dou, Dutch painter
(*dow*)

W.E.B. DuBois, American sociologist
(*duh-boyz*)

Andre Dubus, American fiction writer
(*duh-byoose*)

E

Chiwetel Ejiofor, English actor
(*choo-we-tell edge-ee-oh-for*)

Cary Elwes, American actor
(*ell-wiss*)

Paul Erdős, Hungarian mathematician
(*~pal **ehr**-deush*)

John Scotus Eriugena,
Irish theologian and Neoplatonist
(*era-**jee**-nah*)

Leonhard Euler, German mathematician
(*oiler*)

F

Lee Fang, American journalist
(*fong*)

Nuruddin Farah, Somali novelist
(Somali pronunciation: *~nour-oo-**deen** farr-**ah***)

Colm Feore, Canadian actor
(*column fury*)

Ferdydurke, Gombrowicz novel
(*fair-deh-**dure**-kuh*)

Paul Feyerabend, Austrian philosopher of science
(*fire-**ah**-bent*)

Johann Gottlieb Fichte, German idealist philosopher
(*feesh-tuh*)[2]

**Ralph/Ranulph/Sophie/Joseph/Magnus/
Martha Fiennes**, English actor/explorer/film
director/actor/composer/film director
(*rayf finezzzzzzzzzzzz*)

Gustave Flaubert, French novelist
(*flow-bear*)

William Foege, American epidemiologist
(*fay-ghee*)

Michel Foucault, French Nietzschean philosopher
(*~foo-coh*)

Gottlob Frege, German logician
(*got-lobe free-geh*)

James Frey, American fabulist
(*fry*)

G

Gallaudet University, Washington, D.C.
(*gal-uh-debt*)

---

2   The pronunciation of the *-ch* as soft instead of hard, unlike every
other instance in German, was contrived after the philosopher's death
to avoid a near-homophony with that language's word for 'fuck.'

Clifford Geertz, American anthropologist
  (*gurtz*)

Alberto Giacometti, Swiss sculptor
  (Swiss pronunciation: *yah-coh-**mett**-ee*)[3]

André Gide, French writer
  (*zheed*)

H.R. Giger, Swiss visual artist
  (***ghee**-guh*)

Giotto, Italian painter
  (***jhott**-oh*)

Johann Wolfgang von Goethe, German poet
  (*~**ger**-tuh*)

Nikolai Gogol, Russian fiction writer
  (*goggle*)

Witold Gombrowicz, Polish author and dramatist
  (***vee**-told gomm-**broh**-vitch*)

Jan Gossaert, Flemish painter
  (*~yann **ho**-sight*) aka 'Mabuse' (*mah-**buu**-zuh*)

---

3 Because Giacometti was from the Italian-speaking part of Switzerland a kind of second order snobbishness has descended on the pronunciation of his name. Most people who would judge you pronounce it as you would in Italian (*jah-coh-**mett**-ee*) but an inner-inner circle insist on correcting even these people with the Swiss-Italian pronunciation listed here.

Philip Gourevitch, American journalist
(*guh-**ray**-vitch*)

Antonio Gramsci, Italian Marxist theorist
(***gromm**-she*)

Matt Groening, American cartoonist
(*graining*)

Alexander Grothendieck,
German-French mathematician
(***groat**-enn-deek*)

David Guetta, French DJ
(*gay-tah*)

H

Michael Haneke, Austrian film director
(*hanukkah*)

Vaclav Havel, Czech writer and politician
(***vott**-slav **hah**-vell*)

Margaret H'Doubler, American dancer
(***dough**-blur*)

Seamus Heaney, Irish poet
(***shay**-muss **hee**-knee*)

Aleksandar Hemon, Bosnian-American fiction writer
(between *heh-monn* and *heh-**mown***)

Zbigniew Herbert, Polish poet
(*z'**beeg**-nyeff **herr**-behrt*)

John Hersey, American journalist
(***hearse**-ey*)

Hesiod, Greek poet
(***he**-see-uhd*)

Hermann Hesse, German poet
(*~**hair**-monn **heh**-seh*)

Guy Hocquenghem, French queer theorist
(*ghee **ock**-en-g'yem*)

homo sacer, Agamben concept
(Italian pronunciation: ***oh**-moh **satch**-air*)

Houston Street, Manhattan
(***house**-ton*)

Bohumil Hrabal, Czech fiction writer
(*boh-**who**-meal h'**rah**-ball*)

Alfred Hrdlička, Austrian visual artist
(Austrian pronunciation: *~hairt-**litch**-kah*)

Joris-Karl Huysmans, French novelist
(*~zhour-**ris** karl **weese**-moss*)[4]

I

Jean-Auguste-Dominique Ingres,
French painter and violinist
(*~angh*)

Eugène Ionesco, Romanian dramatist
(Romanian pronunciation: *~yoh-**ness**-koh*)

Luce Irigaray, Belgian-French feminist philosopher
(*loose ear-**ee**-garr-**eh***)

J

Jacques, Shakespeare character
(***jay**-kwiss*)

Roman Jakobson, Russian-American literary theorist
(*jacob-son*)

Erica Jong, American novelist and poet
(*zhong*)

---

4 The last syllable doesn't have an English equivalent but rhymes with
the French pronunciation of *Jean's.*

Seu Jorge, Brazilian musician
(*~sewe zhawzhe*)[5]

Carl Jung, Swiss psychiatrist
(*yoong*)

K

Frigyes Karinthy, Hungarian writer and dramatist
(***free***-*gesh car-**inn**-tee*)

Keble College, Oxford University
(*keeble*)

Kelis Rogers, American singer
(*kuh-**leece***)

Imre Kertész, Hungarian author and Holocaust survivor
(***imm**-reh **kare**-tace*)

John Maynard Keynes, English economist
(*kanes*)

Omar Khayyam, Persian mathematician and polymath
(*high-**yahm***)

Krzysztof Kieślowski, Polish film director
(***krish**-toff keesh-**loff**-skee*)

---

5   Portuguese has a much more complicated phonetics than English
and so this is especially approximate.

Q'orianka/Xihuaru Kilcher, American actor/actor
 (*core-i-an-ka/see-wahr-oo*)

Danilo Kiš, Yugoslav novelist
 (*dann-eel-oh keesh*)

Phil Klay, American fiction writer
 (*kligh*)

Paul Klee, Swiss-German artist
 (*powell clay*)

Stephen Cole Kleene, American mathematician
 (*klain-ee*)

Karl Ove Knausgård, Norwegian author
 (*~kahl oo-veh kuh-nauss-gahd*)

Zoltán Kodály, Hungarian composer
 (*zohwl-tahn koh-die*)

Sarah Koenig, American journalist
 (*kay-nig*)

Alexandre Kojève,
 Russian-French philosopher and civil servant
 (*koh-zhevv*)

Tadeusz Konwicki, Polish author and film director
 (*tah-de-yoosh konn-vitz-ski*)

Jerzy Kosiński, Polish-American novelist
(*yer-zhay koh-shin-ski*)

Alexandre Koyré, Russian-French philosopher of science
(*kwah-ray*)

Saul Kripke, American logician
(*crip-key*)

Thomas Kuhn, American philosopher of science
(*coon*)

Milan Kundera, Czech-French author
(Czech pronunciation: *mill-ahn koon-der-uh*)

L

Henri Lefebvre, French Marxist philosopher
(*luh-fevv-ruh*)

Stanisław Lem, Polish science-fiction writer
(*stan-ni-swaf lemm*)

Jonathan Lethem, American novelist
(*leeth-um*)

Jared Leto, American actor
(*let-oh*)

Primo Levi, Italian chemist, author and Holocaust survivor
(*leh*-*vee*)

Marina Lewycka, Ukrainian-British novelist
(*leh*-**vitz**-*kah*)

Mario Vargas Llosa, Peruvian novelist and politician
(**yoh**-*sah*)

Peter Lorre, German-American actor
(*laura*)

Jan Łukasiewicz, Polish logician
(*yann wu-kah-**shey**-vitch*)

M

Magdalen College, University of Oxford/Cambridge
(**mawd**-*lin*)

Kazimir Malevich,
Russian Suprematist painter and sculptor
(*may-**lay**-vich*)

Thomas Mann, German novelist
(**toe**-*mahs mahn*)

Mannes School of Music, New York City
(*mannis*)

Don Marquis, American editorialist
(*mar-kwiss*)

Quentin Matsys/Quinten Matsijs,
Flemish painter
(Flemish pronunciation: *kvinn-tin mott-sayse*)

Somerset Maugham, English author
(*mawm*)

Olivier Messiaen, French composer
(*oh-leev-yay meh-syonh*)

Joel Meyerowitz, American street photographer
(*my-yer-uh-wits*)

Czesław Miłosz, Polish poet
(*chess-waff me-woahsh*)

Joan Miró, Spanish visual artist
(*zhwamn me-roh*)

László Moholy-Nagy, Hungarian visual artist
(*~lass-low moh-holy noidge-eh*)

Robert Moog, American pioneer of the synthesizer
(*mogue*)

George Mosse, German-American historian
(*mossy*)

Sławomir Mrożek, Polish dramatist
(*swah-**voh**-meer **m'roh**-zhek*)

Ron Mueck, Australian sculptor
(***myoo**-ick*)

Harry Mulisch, Dutch author
(***mool**-ish*)

Edvard Munch, Norwegian painter
(*ed-vart moonk*)

Robert Musil, Austrian novelist
(***moo**-zeal/**moo**-seal*)

Eadweard Muybridge, English photographer
(*edward **my**-bridge*)

N

Nacogdoches, Texas
(*nack-uh-**dough**-chis*)

Natchitoches, Louisiana
(***nack**-uh-tush*)

Otto Neurath, Austrian philosopher
(***noi**-raht*)

Bill Nighy, English actor
  (*nye*)

Anaïs Nin, French memoirist
  (*ah-nayh-**ees** ninn*)

Emmy Noether, German mathematician
  (***neur**-tuh*)

Cees Nooteboom, Dutch novelist
  (*sayze **note**-uh-bome*)

Lupita Nyong'o, Mexican-Kenyan actor
  (*~nnnnn **yong**-oh*)

O

Obergefell v. Hodges, Supreme Court case
  (*oh-**burr**-geh-fell*)

Máirtín Ó Cadhain, Irish novelist
  (***marr**-teen oh **kai**-un*)

Adepero Oduye, American actor
  (***add**-uh-pair-oh oh-**doo**-yay*)

Jenny Offill, American novelist
  (***oh**-full*)

Claes Oldenburg, Swedish-American sculptor
(*kloss*)

Michael Ondaatje, Sri Lankan-Canadian poet
(*awn-**datch**-ee*)

The River Ouse, Sussex
(*ooze*)

David Oyelowo, British-Nigerian actor
(*oh-yell-uh-whoah*)

P

Chuck Palahniuk, American novelist
(***paul**-uh-nik*)

Wolfgang Pauli, Austrian-Swiss physicist
(***pow**-lee*)

Charles Sanders Peirce, American logician
(*purse*)

Samuel Pepys, English diarist
(*peeps*)

Jodi Picoult, American novelist
(***pee**-koh*)

Max Planck, German physicist
    (*plonk*)

Plotinus, Neoplatonist philosopher
    (*ploh-tine-us*)

Anthony Powell, English novelist
    (***po**-uhl*)

John Cowper Powys, English novelist
    (*cooper **poh**-iss*)

Principia Mathematica,
    Newton or Whitehead & Russell treatise
    (*prin-**kipp**-ee-yah*)

Annie Proulx, American fiction writer
    (*proo*)

Marcel Proust, French novelist
    (*proost*)

Joseph Pulitzer, Hungarian-American newspaper baron
    (***puh**-litz-ur*)

Q

Qatar
(*cutter/gutter*)[6]

Quinnipiac University, Hamden, Connecticut
(*kwinn-uh-**pea**-ack*)

R

Ayn Rand, American objectivist author
(***well**-fare recipient*)

Sławomir Rawicz, Polish journalist and Gulag escapee
(*swah-**voh**-meer **rahh**-vitch*)

Satyajit Ray, Indian film director
(Bengali pronunciation: *~**shut**-uh-jeet rye*)

Steve Reich, American minimalist composer
(*raish*)

Tom Regan, American philosopher
(*ray-gun*)

ricercar, musical composition
(Italian pronunciation: *~**reach**-air-car*)

---

6 The first letter (*qaf/qof/*ق) has no equivalent in English or any other Western language, and is more glottal than either of the sounds starting these approximations.

Rainer Maria Rilke, German poet
(*rhine*-er *mahr-ee-a* *reel-kuh*)

Nicolas Roeg, English film director
(*rogue*)

Theodore Roethke, American poet
(*ret*-key)

Wilhelm Conrad Röntgen/Roentgen,
German mechanical engineer and physicist
(*vill*-helm *rhont*-gn)

Klaus Roth, German-British mathematician
(*roath*)

Mary Ruefle, American poet
(*roo*-full)

Ed Ruscha, American visual artist
(*roo*-**shay**)

S

Edward Said, Palestinian-American public intellectual
(*sigh*-**eed**)

Antoine de Saint-Exupéry, French author and aviator
(*sanh-eks-oo*-**pear**-ee)

Luc Sante, American writer
(*sahnt*)

Leonardo Sciascia, Sicilian novelist
(**shah**-*shah*)

Schlumberger, oilfield services company
(**slum**-*burr-zhay*)

Bruno Schulz, Polish author and painter
(*schooltz*)

Martin Scorsese, American film director
(*score-**sess**-ee*)

Henry Scrope, Shakespeare character
(*scroop*)

W.G. Sebald, German-British author
(**zay**-*bald*)

Chloë Sevigny, American actor
(**sevv**-*un-ee*)

Choire Sicha, American blogger and editor
(*corey see-kah*)

Charles Simić, Serbian-American poet
(technically, *simm-**itch*** but often called *simmick*)

Victor Sjöström, Swedish actor
(Swedish pronunciation: *veek-torr hhhwhere-strome*)

Theda Skocpol, American sociologist
(*scotch-pole*)

Josef Škvorecký, Czech-Canadian writer
(*yoh-zeff shkvore-etz-ski*)

William Smellie, Scottish obstetrician
(*smiley*)

Todd Solondz, American film director
(*suh-lawnz*)

Aleksandr Solzhenitsyn, Soviet dissident and historian
(*saul-zhuh-neat-sin*)

Léon Spilliaert, Belgian painter
(Dutch pronunciation: *lay-on spilly-art*)

Edward Steichen,
Luxembourgish-American photographer
(*shtike-inn*)

Strange, barony
(*strang*)

William Stukeley, English archaeologist
(*stoo-key*)

Abbe Suger, French Cluniac statesman
    (French pronunciation: *syoo-zheh*, British: *soo-gehr*)

Wisława Szymborska, Polish poet
    (*vee-swa-va shim-bor-ska*)

T

Gay Talese, American pioneer of New Journalism
    (*tuh-leeze*)

Roger Taney, author of *Dredd Scott* decision
    (*tawny*)

Nahum Tate, Irish poet
    (*neigh-m*)

Tchoupitoulas Street, New Orleans
    (*chop-uh-too-luss*)

Wayne Thiebaud, American painter
    (*tee-bo*)

Uwe Timm/Uwe Timm,
    German writer/German anarchist
    (*ooh-veh*)

Tzvetan Todorov, Bulgarian-French structuralist
    (*tsveh-tahn toh-duh-roff*)

Colm Tóibín, Irish novelist
(Irish pronunciation: ~*column **toh-been***)

Ernst Troeltsch, German Protestant theologian
(*trolch*)

Edward Tufte,
American statistician and graphic designer
(***tuff**-tee*)

Tulane University, New Orleans
(***too**-lane*)

Ivan Turgenev, Russian fiction writer
(*yvonne turr-**gain**-yevv*)

George W. S. Trow, American cultural critic
(rhymes with *grow*)

V

Ludvík Vaculík, Czech dissident writer
(*lood-**veek** **vatz**-oo-**leek***)

Michel Houllebecq, French novelist
(*he doesn't care*)

Joos van Cleve, Netherlandish painter
(*yohss fon **clay**-vuh*)

Arnoldus Vanderhorst,
South Carolina governor and ultimate namesake of
Luther
(*vandross*)

Ludwig Mies van der Rohe,
German-American architect
(***meez** fonn der **roh**-uh*)

Rogier van der Weyden, Flemish painter
(*~ro-**kheer** fon dur **vay**-dun*)

Vincent van Gogh, Dutch painter
(Dutch pronunciation: *~**finch**-ant fan **hawh***)

Antonie van Leeuwenhoek, Dutch microscopist
(*ahn-**toe**-nee fon **lay**-when-hook*)

Rembrandt van Rijn, Dutch painter
(***remm**-brondt fon rain*)

Johannes Vermeer, Dutch painter
(*yo-**hann**-iss furr-**meer***)

Jones Very, American poet
(*jonas veery*)

Vladimir Voinovich, Soviet dissident writer
(*vlah-**dee**-meer voy-**noh**-vitch*)

Ludwig von Mises, Austrian economist
(*fonn **meez**-ess*)

Georg Henrik von Wright,
Finnish analytic philosopher
(*fon vrikt*)

W

Ayelet Waldman, Israeli novelist
(*eye-**yell**-it*)

Quvenzhané Wallis, American actor
(*kwuh-**ven**-zhuh-nay*)

Robert Walser, Swiss novelist
(*valzer*)

Jean-Antoine Watteau, French painter
(French pronunciation: *~vah-toh*)

Evelyn St. John Waugh, English novelist
(***eve**-linn **sin**-jun wahh*)

Max Weber, German sociologist
(***veigh**-burr*)

Simone/André Weil,
French philosopher/mathematician
(*zee-**moan** veigh*)

Elie Wiesel,
Romanian-American writer and Holocaust survivor
(***eel**-ee vee-**zell***)

Garry Winogrand, American photographer
(***win**-uh-grand*)

Ludwig Wittgenstein, Austrian-British philosopher
(***vitt**-genn-shtein*)

Pelham Grenville Wodehouse, English novelist
(***wood**-house*)

David Wojnarowicz, American visual artist
(*voy-nah-**roh**-vitch*)

Hermann Wouk, American novelist
(*woke*)

Woyzeck, Büchner play
(***voight**-zikk*)

Joseph Wright of Derby, English painter
(*right of **dahr**-bee*)

Y

William Butler Yeats, Irish poet
   (*yates*)

Yerkes Observatory, Williams Bay, Wisconsin
   (**yer**-*keys*)

Yoknapatawpha County, Faulkner setting
   (*yolk-nuh-pah-**taw**-fa*)

Z

Robert Zajonc, American psychologist
   (**zai**-*unts*)

Slavoj Žižek, Slovenian psychoanalytic philosopher
   (**slah**-*voi* **zhee**-*zhek*)

Andrzej Żuławski, Polish film director
   (*ahn-drey zhu-**wavv**-ski*)

ALS NICK KAN